A Tenth of a Second
To Live

Norvin "Bud" Evans

To: Bill

An adventure I could have done without in my long flight got career

N. E. 'Bud' Evans

Other Books & Publications by Norvin "Bud" Evans

When Should You Believe Landing Gear Lights?
By Norvin C. Evans
—Test Flying At Old Wright Field

Aviating With Evans, An Experimental Test Pilot
By Norvin "Bud" Evans
ISBN No.: 978-0-9963066-8-3, Paperback, 478 pages,
Blue Note Publications, Inc., 2016

Reviews for "Aviating With Evans":

"I really enjoyed this book. It is a very good read! "Bud" Evans had one heck of an aviation career, as a combat pilot flying the P-80 in Korea to some very interesting (and exciting) experimental test pilot work flying a wide variety of the Air Force's newest aircraft. I think, like me, you will have a hard time putting this one down. Several of the stories in the book are of the "Holy cow, did he really do that and survive?" variety. When you get to them, you will know what they are. Good job, Bud, and thanks for your above and beyond service to our country."

—Francis L. Kapp, Col. USAF (Ret)
Daedalus, Spring & Summer 2017

5.0 out of 5 stars
Bud Knocks it Out of the Park!!
"The history in this book is astounding. If you enjoy aerospace history in any form, this is a must read. Bud has been everywhere in the Golden Age of Test flight and the past comes to life!!!"

—By The Florida Reviewer on May 9, 2016

5.0 out of 5 stars
"Check out how many different types of aircraft he flight tested and lived to write about it - Congrats!"
"This is a must read book for any one who likes aviation. Mr. Evans is a person of integrity and did so much during his aviation career. This book should be on the top of the list! I wish him the best of the best!"

—By Wizard on July 15, 2016

A Tenth of a Second
To Live

Norvin "Bud" Evans

BLUE NOTE
PUBLICATIONS, INC.

Copyright ©2018 Norvin C. Evans

All rights reserved. No part of this book may be used or reproduced in any manner whatsoever without written permission of the publisher or author except in the case of brief quotations embodied in critical articles or reviews.

SecondPrinting

Melbourne, Florida

Blue Note Publications, Inc.

1-800-624-0401

Library of Congress Control Number: 2018934590

ISBN No.: 978-0-9977638-9-8

The stories in this book are the author's own personal experiences, reported as he saw them. The opinions of the author on the people, places and events are only the author's observations and opinions.

*

Printed In The United States of America

Without the help and support of my family this book would never have been written:

My patient wife Nancy.

Sarah Gkonos who was instrumental in organizing and editing the manuscript with help from her fiancé Adam.

My daughter, Tracy Gkonos, whose patient editing was a great help in getting this manuscript to the publisher.

PROLOGUE

This book has been written to tell the story of one of many dedicated Americans who conducted seriously hazardous jobs for the benefit of the United States. They did their job with the full knowledge that they would never receive credit or recognition for their sacrifices if they survived the task. Those aircrews that participated in hydrogen bomb tests on Bikini and Eniwetok Atolls during Operation Redwing in 1956 portray a good example of one of the highly classified test programs by dedicated Americans. This book is dedicated to those unsung heroes.

FOREWORD

This is the story of a life changing experience that had an impact on me and all of those test pilots and crews who were selected to perform a very dangerous and frustrating task that required living for five and one-half months on a tiny atoll in the South Pacific. We all knew that we were flying into extremely dangerous nuclear bomb explosions to determine what size bomb our aircraft could deliver and still have a reasonable chance of escaping without catastrophic damage.

There were a couple of reasons I decided to keep this journal of my life on this top-secret classified experience: One: I had failed to do so during my two combat tours in the Korean War, and Two: because there was so little else to spend time on when I wasn't flying. I knew that everything we were doing as far as our flying was concerned would be highly classified, so my journal was locked away for over 50 years. My wife Evie and two daughters did not know what I was actually doing in those months that we were separated. Evie passed away 23 years after the tests and never knew exactly what I was doing during our almost six month separation.

More than once in my flying career I have been sent on flights where I knew the chance of my survival was very low. This story is about the most harrowing of those occasions. It became obvious after flying my first mission on Operation Redwing that someone was willing to sacrifice me in order to get the data they needed. On my first mission of the five-and-a-half month long test project I had received more radiation exposure than anyone ever should have. However, there was no one trained to do my job and the powers in charge couldn't get the needed data without exposing me to much more than the allowable amount. I was ordered to continue for six more bomb tests where I was positioned closer than any pilot has ever been to hydrogen bomb explosions.

This story is partially written from the diary notes I kept hidden for 50 years and takes the reader through the happy, sad, fun and frustrating events that were my experiences before, during, and after those life defining months on that isolated, overcrowded atoll known as Eniwetok.

Eniwetok is a large atoll located in the South Pacific and is part of the Marshall Islands. It is also where the United States conducted its nuclear bomb testing from 1948 to 1958. The atoll was home to about 3,000 men during my stay. The company Holmes and Narver was responsible for the basic services such as feeding, facility maintenance, etc. The Air Force provided air support and test aircraft. The Army was responsible for security. The Navy provided surface transportation to test sites and facilities and there was some part of all U.S. military involved in support of Operation Redwing.

Our test team consisted of a B-52, B-47, B-66, B-57B, F-101A and two F-84F's. The Navy provided an A-3D. Each aircraft was positioned directly over the bomb's blast, but at different altitudes based on the structural limits of the aircraft. As my F-84F was the strongest aircraft in the U.S. military, I was always placed in the closest position relative to the bomb's explosion. The other F-84F was placed off to the side of the blast so as to measure side loads affect on the aircraft.

The only indication that the pilot had as to the force of the shock wave from the bomb was the number registered on the aircraft's g-force meter. The force of the bomb's shock wave was an instantaneous force with no buildup from 1g to whatever is registered on the g-force meter. Aircraft structural limits were determined at the factory by putting force on the aircraft's airframe until some major structure failed. That determined what g-force the aircraft could survive and therefore determined the published structural limits while operating the aircraft. There was no testing done to determine instantaneous force impacting the aircraft structure such as was created by the hydrogen bomb blast. The force that hit the aircraft from the bomb's blast was instantaneous, which the aircraft designers did not take into consideration when designing and building the aircraft.

Come join me in my adventure from days of boredom to moments of stark terror where death was only a tenth of a second away!

—Norvin "Bud" Evans

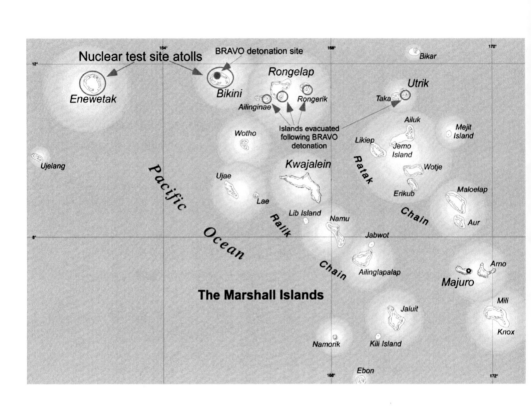

CONTENTS

Prologue 7

Foreword 9

Eniwetok And The Bomb 15

Off To The South Pacific 29

The Trip 37

Eniwetok Atoll 49

Back On The Island 65

The First Live Mission 73

The Bomb's First Light 87

The Beat Goes On 95

No Relief In Sight 139

Off To Edwards 159

Return To Edwards 161

The Rest Of The Story 169

Epilogue 201

Glosssary 203

"They had the task of designing and installing a 'space positioning system' that would allow me to fly to a point in space with an error tolerance of +/- 1/10 of a second. I smiled, as most pilots would, when I read the tolerance requirements, feeling certain that they were unrealistic limits. Any fighter test pilot knew that even though we could 'walk on water' no one could fly a high speed, unstable aircraft to those finite limits. Little did I know that in order to get the needed data and survive, I would have to hit that point in space, within that timeframe, seven different times and to my surprise, I was able to do it."

ENIWETOK AND THE BOMB

It was the first true flight test program which I was offered as my own test project and there was no way I would refuse it.

January 1955

Major R. D. Hunt, Chief of the Fighter Test Division, Wright Air Development Center (WADC), Wright-Patterson AFB, Ohio knew without question that as a newly assigned graduate of the Air Force Test Pilot School at Edwards AFB I would be surprised and delighted to have a flight test program offered to me so soon after arriving for my first test pilot job. Normally it took a year or more to be assigned your first full project and some test pilots never were given a complete test program that was theirs alone. I accepted the challenge without any questions, even after being told only that it would be a very demanding and high-risk project. After my pre-assumed acceptance, R. D. told me that it had to do with flying into nuclear bomb blasts and that I would have to await my special security clearance before I would be given any more information.

I had arrived at Wright-Patterson a few months before and had checked out in every type aircraft that our fighter test division owned. I was flying on 12 different test projects, which was normal, considering we had as many as 100 projects assigned to the 22 test aircraft that we had. Some of the "flying test beds," as most of our machines were designated, would have as many as six different test projects assigned to one aircraft. Our primary job as the fighter test operations at the Wright Air Development Center (WADC) was to support the various engineering and research labs, which made up most of the Center's function for the Air Force. These various labs conceived new ideas for tactics, hardware, software or a need to validate a system designed by civilian industry to be used by the U.S. Air Force. The lab would then work with the Flight Test Group to determine how and on what type aircraft it could be installed and tested. We constantly had aircraft in the modification shops and some of the configuration changes took more than a year to complete. They often came back to us having very little resemblance to the aircraft that it had originally been designed and built to be.

We had no standard aircraft and although some looked the same as the operational models, the cockpits and internal systems were all different. These test systems and the switches to operate them made it necessary to change the normal cockpit switch positions, add new ones plus special test instrumentation panels. This required performance and stability flight tests on each aircraft as it came out of the modification shops. The degree of aerodynamic flight-testing varied according to the type of basic changes made to the original design of the airframe and engine. This was done before testing the system that was installed in the aircraft could begin. Although we had several F-86's, F-84's, F-94's, etc. a pilot checkout was required in each and every airplane because of the total differences between every one of them.

Checkout on the test systems was also required for each pilot flying the test. The airplanes often carried test panels and systems onboard that were inactive, awaiting test data to be evaluated or system redesign to correct deficiencies discovered during flight-testing. Often when a program was completed the equipment would be left on the aircraft until such time when the other test system or systems were completed or the test cancelled. The time to remove test systems in most cases took longer than it did to install them and in both cases the paperwork required was unbelievable. A great deal of our time was spent becoming familiar with the many different test requirements and their associated systems. No other flying organization, including Edwards AFB, required a pilot to fly and be completely familiar with as many "one of a kind" aircraft. Although most pilots graduating from the test pilot school wanted to stay at Edwards, I found my assignment at Dayton very challenging and satisfying.

When I graduated from the school, there was only one fighter slot available at Edwards and that was pre-assigned to Captain Mel Apt who had been flying with Fighter Test at Dayton prior to coming to the test pilot school. He was later killed in the X-2 just after he set a new speed record.

There was very little time to waste on ceremony when I arrived at WADC. I was fortunate that my own squadron executive officer from the 9th Fighter Squadron in Japan and Korea, Clyde Good, was the Executive Officer of the Fighter Test Operations section. He was a big help in getting me past the "new boy" treatment and put me right to work. I had flown most of the standard fighters in the Air Force prior to being assigned to WADC so it was easy to start right in on the less demanding tests, being familiar with the basic aircraft's flying characteristics.

Most of the tests that I flew early in my testing career were assigned to other pilots as their projects, but most of the test pilots participated in other pilot's projects at some point during the program. Some of these test projects were: The All Magnesium F-80; the F-89, F86, and F-94 TACAN project; the T-33, and F-94B Ejection Seat Test-Bed. Other projects were the F-86 Automatic Instrument Landing Auto-Pilot; the F-84G and F-86D Windshield Anti-Rain Systems; the F-86D Fly-By-Wire Flight Control Systems project; the Light Weight Fighter Radar System project and many others.

My tasks associated with the H-Bomb tests were fairly limited at first and required very little time away from my regular daily flight-testing duties. First I was given a few general briefings as to where I would be flying: namely the base at Eniwetok (an atoll that is part of the Marshall Islands in the south Pacific Ocean and the target area at Bikini) where most of the test bombs would explode. The aircraft assigned to me was being earmarked at the factory and would be the latest model F-84F, which was the F-84F-25. It incorporated a lot of system changes and some major airframe/flight control changes from the earlier model F-84F. There were a few modifications made in the instrument and electronic systems to replace the normal weapon systems that would be installed on the other aircraft on the production line. When mine came off the production line it was delivered directly to a laboratory that installed special test recording instrumentation by an electronics research company.

They had the task of designing and installing a "space positioning system" that would allow me to fly to a point in space with an error tolerance of +/- 1/10 of a second. I smiled, as most pilots would, when I read the tolerance requirements, feeling certain that they were unrealistic limits. Any fighter test pilot knew that even though we could "walk on water" no one could fly a high speed, unstable aircraft to those finite limits. Little did I know that in order to get the needed data and survive, I would have to hit that point in space, within that timeframe, seven different times and to my surprise, I was able to do it.

I'm getting ahead of my story and I'll come back to my Wright-Patterson AFB routine. It was more than a year from the time I was assigned to the Eniwetok project until I had to leave for the islands.

I hadn't flown the F-84F and needed a checkout before going to Florida to test the new space positioning system designated "Radist." We didn't have an F-84F in operation, although we had several of the older models being modified for other test projects. A few weeks after being assigned to the program (later code-named "Redwing") an F-84F came out of the modification shop, and I was scheduled to checkout in it after it had undergone the required functional check flight by a qualified pilot. All of our aircraft were single pilot machines. The day I was scheduled to fly the checkout flight in the F-84F-25 I also checked out in the F-94C. As a matter of fact, I wasn't aware that the F-84 was available until after I had landed from my flight in the F-94C.

To give you a little better understanding as to how we had to checkout in our specially configured aircraft (which would curl the hair of most military pilots) the routine was as follows: First, you read the pilots' handbook that described the production model of the type aircraft. Then you read all of the change documents for each of the test systems installed on the particular aircraft you were to fly on your checkout flight. There were instructor pilots, usually the project pilot assigned to each aircraft, who were responsible for briefing the pilot being checked-out in his assigned aircraft. This would cover the cockpit switches, aircraft system changes, and instruments. He would then stand on the ladder and supervise the engine start procedure and check that the systems were all correct for take-off before the pilot taxied out from the ramp. The instructor pilot then returned to operations and listened to the radio to follow the flight and be available to offer any verbal assistance if needed.

In the case of my checkout in the F-84F I met with the Republic Aircraft Company technical representative and the instructor pilot, Captain Tracy Mathewson, and he gave me a thorough briefing on the F-84F. My flight profile included a climb to well over 40,000 feet and a steep dive through Mach 1(exceeding the speed of sound) to experience its handling qualities in supersonic flight. The F-84F would only reach supersonic flight in a steep dive.

After take-off I performed some basic handling maneuvers and then climbed to 45,000 feet where the aircraft handling was very sloppy and the rate of climb was almost zero. I rolled the F-84 inverted, eased back smoothly on the stick, staying just above the heavy stall buffet until the nose was at about a 45-degree dive angle. I then rolled 180 degrees, and pointed the nose toward the ground with the throttle full open. At a speed just below supersonic the Mach meter hesitated at about .96 Mach and the aircraft had a pronounced wing roll and nose tuck. Suddenly the aircraft responded to my controls, the Mach meter jumped to 1.02 and I was hurdling toward the Earth above the speed of sound.

This didn't last for more than 10 seconds or so because, as I descended at a high rate into more dense air, I could feel the nose tuck and wing roll again. A check of the Mach meter confirmed that I was sub-sonic again. My indicated speed was still very high and I was barreling toward terra firma at a frightening rate. Having been briefed to make a 6g pullout, I pulled back on a very stiff, resisting stick. Approaching 6g's I experienced a sudden "bang" accompanied by a violent rolling, pitching, and yawing of the aircraft.

My automatic reaction was to relax stick pressure, retard the throttle to idle, open the speed brakes, and check the instrument panel. This was intuitive, but there is always that heart stopping moment that brings all your senses to a sharp "alert" when something unexpected threatens life and limb, particularly in an unfamiliar aircraft.

I was relieved to feel that I could control the aircraft, indicating that I had not lost a major part of the airframe. There on the instrument panel were several amber and red warning lights glaring at me indicating a loss of hydraulic pressure, and the landing gear red unsafe light was illuminated in the gear handle. The left main landing gear indicator showed "down and locked," the nose gear indicator showed "up and locked," and the right main gear indicated "unsafe."

After a quick assessment of my predicament and having flown the aircraft into a nose high climbing attitude to slow down to a safe "gear down" speed, I called Flight Ops on the radio to inform Tracy of my condition. I noted that both hydraulic warning lights were on but I was showing some pressure on the flight control system. I couldn't see the right landing gear and wasn't sure whether it was up, down or completely departed from the aircraft. I was about 20 miles from Patterson Field and at about 20,000 feet, so I suggested that I make a pass by the tower for a visual check as to my landing gear status. Tracy's reply was to the affirmative, but seconds later his voice came back on the radio with more than a little anxiety in it, advising me to come straight in and land as soon as possible. I explained that I might not have a landing gear on the right side. He replied that the Republic Tech had advised him that there was a possibility that I would lose all my flight control systems and to waste no time getting on the ground even with only one main gear.

Easy for him to say! The F-84F that I was flying had two hydraulic systems, which supplied fluid to the flight controls. One indicated zero pressure and the other showed some pressure but much lower than normal. The fact that my flight control pressure had dropped to 2200 PSI is the thing that caused the concern to those on the ground. From my vantage (or disadvantage) point, I could tell that I had sloppy response to the movements of the control stick and that the system definitely was not reacting to the situation as advertised.

The thought of landing a high-performance fighter that I had never been in before without landing flaps or wheel brakes and a sluggish stick response was anything but ideal. Add the fact that I didn't know and wouldn't be allowed to find out whether I had a right landing gear or nose gear until I touched down on the concrete runway, if I could reach it before losing the rest of my flight controls, was also a concern. I had placed the gear handle in the down position and had felt the drag increase, telling me the nose gear had at least come part way down. The indicator still showed "up and locked." My briefing before the flight instructed me after take-off to return the gear handle to the neutral position after the gear indicators showed "up and locked" and the red light in the gear handle went out. This was done to take the pressure off the hydraulic system. Of course the chance of causing a hydraulic leak was reduced by not keeping the high pressure on that system during the time it was securely locked in the up position. This procedure was different from all the other fighters, but the explanation made sense to me and I assumed it was due to hydraulic leaking problems with F-84F's in the past.

Regardless of the reasons, it was obvious to me that the up-locks hadn't held through the 6g pull-out and now I was going to have to land on one wheel, two wheels, or hopefully three wheels. Even knowing this, I had to hope that the flight control pressure would allow me enough control to make a landing on the left main gear smoothly enough to hold the nose and right gear (if there was one) off the runway. I could then slowly lower the right wing and then the nose to hopefully touch on the runway. (Note—all of this without ever having made a landing in an F-84F type of aircraft before).

I made my straight-in approach and found my ability to control the aircraft more difficult as I slowed my speed. The normal approach speed with landing flaps would have been about 140-150 knots, but without flaps and at heavy weight I was shooting for 200 knots. That, I hoped, would give me a little better control and allow me sufficient airspeed to hold the nose and right wing high while making a soft touch down with the left wheel. I added a few extra knots for the wife and children. At least I thought I had.

It's moments like this when pilots' skills reach razor edge

sharpness and they perform at their absolute best. Those that don't aren't around very long in the test business and those who cannot, don't survive. That isn't a pat on my back but it is a well-known fact among old time test pilots. At that time I had a lot of unknowns to deal with and very little room for miscalculation. It is also a time when I was glad I had learned to fly by "the seat of my pants." I called on past experience and a feeling of being part of the aircraft, although I had just begun to feel the handling responses of this F-84F.

As I started a six-mile final approach, I switched to the Patterson Control Tower. They had already been alerted as to my predicament by Tracy and had cleared traffic from the pattern. The runway threshold was so far from the tower that they couldn't tell me whether my gear was down, even with their binoculars. The main runway at Patterson was 10,000 feet long plus 1,000 feet overruns on each end and this made the task a lot easier for me. I knew the end of the runway had a barrier that could stop me if I couldn't stop by the time I reached the far end of the concrete.

Just before my left gear touched the ground, the Tower called to tell me the nose gear looked like it was down but they couldn't see the right gear. That was hardly comforting, but I had already committed myself to my one shot try and greased the left wheel onto the runaway holding the right wing up as long as I could. Keeping the nose high was not a problem, so as I reached full left stick, I let the right wing drop and lowered the nose slowly to have as much control as I could. If the right gear was not there or if it was there and collapsed as the weight of the aircraft settled on it, it was not going to be much fun!

To my great relief and surprise, I felt the right gear touch and hold, keeping me heading straight down toward the far end of the runway. The nose was eased down and held. In fact, the nose gear indicator indicated "down and locked" as soon as it touched the ground. Relieved by my good fortune, I allowed the F-84 to roll straight ahead until it came to a stop, followed by an entourage of fire and crash vehicles with red lights flashing. I left the engine running to keep any pressure I might have in the hydraulic system in order to hold the landing gear in the "down" position, as many years of experience had taught me.

Even though I was sure the right gear was safe to taxi on, I knew there was no need to take a chance. I sat on the end of the runway and waited for the ground crew to arrive to put the ground locking pins in the three landing gears. Several cars from the maintenance and Ops arrived and Tracy looked up to indicate that everything looked okay. I was really relieved until I noticed everyone beginning to crowd around the right wing. In a minute, the maintenance officer gave me a finger across the throat signal telling me to shut down the engine. After securing the cockpit switches and putting the safety pins in the ejection seat, I climbed down the ladder, which had been placed up to the cockpit.

The group crowded around the right landing gear noticed me as I approached them and began to make comments as to the luck and skill that had accompanied my landing. A quick look at the position of the landing gear strut angle was all I needed to understand what they meant. It should have been perpendicular to the ground being, held in that position by a hydraulic actuating rod and a "stop pad" built onto the main spar of the wing. Instead, the gear was angled approximately 15 degrees outboard of the vertical with the actuating arm dangling in two pieces. The cylinder was hanging from the wheel well and still attached to the wing and the push rod. Having pulled completely out of the cylinder, it was dangling toward the ground from the landing gear strut. The tire was in strips of frazzled ribbons, having rolled along on the inside portion as the aircraft settled with all its weight on the free-floating strut.

I knew then that I had lucked out and my first ever F-84F touchdown had been as perfect as I had hoped it would be. With the gear dangling free, my easing of the right wing down toward the runway had allowed the wheel to contact the concrete at 90 degrees thus holding the weight of the aircraft. As I slowed down on the rollout to a stop, the gear had slowly started to move outboard. It had been prevented from completely collapsing by the forward momentum and friction of the tire on the ground. Had the touchdown not been exactly right, the gear would have folded inside or outboard, ruining my whole day.

As it was, very few people knew about the incident because it was well after quitting time and only the crew on my F-84 and Tracy were there. Of course, the base emergency crews and flight safety officer came out to the aircraft after the landing but on a base as large as Wright-Patterson, it went unnoticed except for those few of us involved. I had a flight and incident report to write. Tracy and I then stopped at the bar with the tech-rep and the maintenance officer, Major Brown, for a martini.

Shortly after writing my incident report, a new procedure requiring the landing gear handle to be left in the "up" position during flight was issued to all F-84F-25 pilots. That was my introduction to the aircraft I was to be flying in the "H" bomb tests. Incidentally, the aircraft had to have the wing replaced as the "down stop" was a forged part of the main spar and had broken off at the impact of the gear snapping down at such a tremendous force.

"The Snark was a missile that took off from a runway while being flown by remote control and was designed to fly for a long distance. When it reached its pre-determined Initial Point (I.P.), it detached its engine/airframe from the warhead, which then went ballistic. My job was to fly over the launch runway at Cape Canaveral AFB, pick up the Snark and its control aircraft on take-off, fly on its wing and photograph it through a camera mounted inside the fuselage of the aircraft I was flying."

OFF TO THE SOUTH PACIFIC

March, 1956

During the following months and prior to leaving for the Pacific paradise, I made several trips to Patrick AFB, Florida to fly the aircraft system "Radist" that I was to use for five-and-a-half months flying out of Eniwetok. There were many problems with the development of the Radist system and I had to spend as many as four weeks at a time in that mosquito haven. The Radist project engineer from WADC was a young lieutenant named Bob Mercer, and he had a car that he had picked up from someone who was leaving Patrick Air Force Base. I don't think he paid much for it as I kidded him saying the only thing holding it together was the rust. However, it was good to have it for transportation on that lonely base. Without a car, we were trapped.

Bob was assigned to the Radist Company on a long term Temporary Duty (TDY) and needed a car. The per-diem I was paid while staying on a military base was $5.00 per day, not allowing money to rent a car for those of us who were only there for a few days at a time. The Officers Club was in a beautiful location right on the ocean but the quality of food was unbelievably poor. I nicknamed Bob's car as the "rust mobile," but it was nice to have it to get away from the base. It always cost me money to live when I was away from home on Air Force business. Even on the base it cost more than the $5.00 to eat and pay for the Visiting Officers Quarters (V.O.Q.) room. (Sometime after I retired from the service, they changed their philosophy and made the per-diem reasonably close to the actual cost of living while you were away from home, but that was never the case while I was on active duty.)

I was very unhappy with my first stay at Patrick AFB because I spent so much time waiting for the test system to be corrected after each of the few flights I was able to fly on the test aircraft. When I was scheduled to go back to Patrick for more development test flights, I worked it so that I could take our F-86 or F-100 photo and pacer aircraft to fly support missions for the Northrop Snark Missile Program being conducted at Patrick. That made the waiting time for the Radist aircraft a little more productive.

The Snark was a missile that took off from a runway while being flown by remote control and was designed to fly for a long distance. When it reached its pre-determined Initial Point (I.P.), it detached its engine/airframe from the warhead, which then went ballistic. My job was to fly over the launch runway at Cape Canaveral AFB, pick up the Snark and its control aircraft on take-off, fly on its wing and photograph it through a camera mounted inside the fuselage of the aircraft I was flying. On the slow speed tests, we used the F-86 and for the high-speed flights we used the F-100. The "Pacer" requirement was to calibrate the airspeed and altitude system on the Snark. These chase flights required close formation on racetrack patterns with the Snark, and then follow it in for its landing. These were sometimes more than a little interesting if not discouraging.

The Northrop chase aircraft was an F-89 named the "Scorpion" because its profile with the fat center portion where the twin tandem cockpits above the two Allison J-35 engines were located. The skinny boom-like aft fuselage, with its tall tail section, gave the definite appearance of that poisonous arachnid with the same name. It was manned by a remote control pilot in the back seat, which flew the missile while it was in the air. There was also a remote control station at the far end of the runway with a pilot who controlled the Snark's take-offs and landings. I would join up with the missile and the control aircraft after take-off, get the airspeed and altitudes and then fly on the control ship's wing while he would bring it in for the landing.

This was the exciting part to watch and although I had no official function, I enjoyed watching the skill exercised by the control team during this phase of the flight. It took a great deal of talent and coordination and it was no easy job. There were a number of failures that occurred during and shortly after take-off that caused the Atlantic waters just off Cape Canaveral to be known as "Snark infested waters." At one point, there were enough problems with the missile just after take-off that they had me stay on the ground at Patrick until they were in the air and the systems were "all up" before calling for me to take-off.

I would have the aircraft running and at the end of the runway waiting for a "go" or "no-go" call.

As we got further into the program and the system became fairly reliable, I would chase the Snark in the F-100 because of its high-speed capability. The F-89 could stay with the missile on the slower test flights but could not stay with it at the operational high-speed end of the mission profile, which included separating the warhead nose section from the main airframe/engine section. This was another exciting exercise for the photo chase and it took every bit of self-discipline I could muster to film it. The system was designed so that at the separation point where the warhead became a ballistic missile, explosive bolts connecting the airframe to the warhead were fired to cause separations. At the same moment, the controls of the aircraft portion went to full nose up and hard right roll positions. The unfortunate part of this system from my perspective was the pacer aircraft, both the F-86 and F-100 had the cameras mounted inside the left side of the fuselage and of course the camera sight was installed on the left canopy rail. This meant that on all photography flights it was necessary to fly on the right wing of whatever you were photographing.

There were no problems until the time of separation when the cameras had to be focused on the mid-ship of the Snark where the explosive bolts were located in order to record their firing and then follow the warhead down as far as you could. This required my rolling toward the missile as it descended towards its target. The F-100 couldn't dive quickly enough or fly fast enough to stay with the missile so I had to maneuver the aircraft anyway I could to accomplish the task. The part that was really hairy was flying in close formation with a "bird," which was at least as large as mine, while concentrating on keeping the separation section riveted in the camera sight. All the time you knew that when the bolts fired, that large airframe/engine was going to roll hard right directly into you while pulling up at the same time. I also knew that you must start a rolling descent to the left in order to keep the warhead in your sights. Such was the demand for concentration just to keep your cameras trained on the warhead. To add to that, the point in space where the separation occurred was well out of sight of land and not a very hospitable area in which to bailout.

These missions filled some of the time between flights in the F-84F that was to become almost a part of me during the time I was to spend flying off of that isolated atoll in the South Pacific. My trips in my F-84F Radist airplane consisted of flying "down range" from Patrick AFB to the Grand Bahamas Island where I made a low pass down the runway of the Air Force tracking station on the east end of the island. I would then climb to ten thousand feet out to the east for ten miles, crossing a line perpendicular to a calibration station on the mainland. I would then climb to a pre-planned test altitude, which varied from flight to flight, and fly a two-legged portion of what would be a triangle. That was leaving the return leg representing the run from Bikini back to Eniwetok out, as that was not to be required as a Radist positioning function. The point in space that we used represented the point over Bikini at "time zero" was located on the Melbourne Airport about eight miles from the Patrick runway. The base on Grand Bahamas represented the take-off point from Eniwetok and the course from there varied slightly according to the test results of the previous flight.

Each of the flights seemed to be accurate, at least from the cockpit, when the system didn't fail, although very hard to fly. I was impressed when I saw data showing how close the system was coming to the "ground zero" spot. However, when I looked at the overlays of the spot where it should have placed me and where I actually was, I realized that it was not meeting the tight tolerance requirements. If I was to survive the bomb blasts then it was "back to the drawing boards" for those truly talented engineers at Radiation Corporation, the company that developed "Radist," as they had what seemed to me to be an impossible requirement to meet. After each of these failures, I either kept on flying photo chase missions if they were needed; sat around to fly the next Radist test flight, if it was forecast to be ready within a few days; or flew back to "Wright's Pasture" to resume the test programs I had been participating in at the home base.

There were some very interesting programs that I was flying and I didn't like to stay away for too long on these TDY's (Temporary Duty). One in particular was the comparison combat performance evaluation of the MIG-15 vs. the F-86F. I was flying the F-86 and after the first half of the evaluation was completed, I was to fly the MIG and repeat the same test with the other pilot flying the F-86. We had completed the first half and while I was on one of my Patrick AFB TDY's an order came from USAF Headquarters. The order directed us at WADC (Wright Air Development Center) to give a checkout flight to a high-ranking RAF officer. The officer was stationed at the British Embassy in Washington. He apparently had swung the deal at a D.C. cocktail party with someone looking for a favor or repaying a favor previously received. Whatever the reason, the RAF pilot stalled the MIG-15 about 50 feet above the runway on his first landing attempt, hitting the concrete so hard that he drove the landing gear struts up through the wings. This ended my chance to fly the MIG-15. It also added another data point in my disillusionment with politicians using their power to impress people and destroying our assigned job and in this case, to take advantage of the tax dollars paid to the North Korean pilot to acquire the MIG.

There were three good things about the program: The assignment of Lt. Mercer to stay with the project at Radiation Corporation in Melbourne, making certain that the system was really ready for test flights before sending me down. The second was that Capt. Charles "Kitch" Kitchens, who was to be using the same system in another F-84F, was sent in my place whenever I was tied up in the middle of a test program at Wright-Patterson. Lastly and most happily was the fact that the system was being "fine-tuned" and required only small refinements making the scheduled aircraft/system tests more realistic.

Kitch was a Los Angeles native as was his wife, Wanda. He was a good-looking man and would have made a good Hollywood image of a fighter test pilot. Not only that but he was also an excellent pilot and we enjoyed each other's companionship in our flying duties. We were also drinking buddies and remained good friends right up to his untimely death. I was the last person to see him alive, with the exception of Brack Harold who was with him in the Lockheed-12, which Kitch owned. He left the Air Force shortly after he returned from Eniwetok and joined the F-104 flight test organization at Palmdale, California, just 45 miles from Edwards Air Force Base, where I was assigned shortly after I returned from Eniwetok. We flew together as before, while I was flying test F-104's at Edwards and Palmdale, and I flew chase flights on some of his test missions. We attended joint meetings and still partied together on a regular basis. He eventually became the Chief F-104 test pilot for Lockheed. I climbed off Kitch's Lockheed-12 just before he took off from the Quartz Hill Airport near Palmdale on his last and final flight.

I miss him and his carefree personality the same way I miss many of our fun-loving group of close-knit test pilots who are no longer with us—but that's another story.

The last three trips to Florida that I made were just before the final time constraints dictating when the Radist system was to be delivered to Cook Laboratories in Chicago, Illinois for the final airframe and engine instrumentation installation. The airframe of my test F-84F had thermocouples and strain gauges attached to every metal skin panel and structural strut in the entire aircraft. In addition, there were special over-pressure sensors located throughout the tailpipe and engine sections. From there the aircraft was delivered to the Port at Oakland, California to be cocooned and placed on a Navy "CVE" aircraft carrier for transport to Eniwetok. On my last working day at the office before leaving with Kitch, I flew a test mission in an F-86F, another in an F-94C, and a functional (maintenance) check flight in an F-100A. We had a nice weekend with the normal flight test parties and the dinner party with families and friends to send us off in style and have some time with our children. (Many half-joking remarks about the Last Supper were naturally enjoyed by all but our wives.)

THE TRIP

We departed Dayton on February 24, 1956 on a TWA commercial flight to San Francisco, California and then by staff car to Travis Air Force Base (between Oakland and Sacramento, California). We arrived late in the afternoon and like all good fighter pilots, we carried our helmets in padded zipper topped olive drab helmet bags. These we carried with us on the airliner, as you would never trust it to baggage handlers of the airlines. One of the few perks given to Air Force test pilots was the custom made "Lombard" pilot's helmet. It was treated with extreme care and was your "status symbol." No other monetary or career enhancing benefits came from being a test pilot in the Air Force for several reasons: You were out of the mainstream of operational or staff requirements. Second, very few, if anyone, on the promotion board knew what the coded job title M.O.S. meant (Military Operational Specialty code-codes used to identify particular jobs). Third, there were so few of us that you were unlikely to find a sponsor to help you on the board. The monetary benefits were also non-existent as you received the same pay as the "desk jockey" who flew his four hours a month in a nice safe C-47 or other such aircraft. That is one of the reasons so many of our group left the service to work for the civilian aircraft companies who paid good salaries and bonuses for flight-testing. The irony was that those salaries and bonuses were paid by the military as part of the contracts for the aircraft being built for them.

At Travis, we had a light load as far as clothing was concerned. We had sent our flying gear, (except for the helmet) along with our personal equipment specialist on board the B-52 test aircraft that was flown over by its crew, along with the B-47, B-57, and B-66 that were also being flown over by their crews. We threw our bags into an assigned VOQ (Visiting Officers Quarters) room and reported to the transportation office at the (Military Air Transport Service) MATS passenger terminal on the flight line.

After going through the processing line, we were assigned to leave the next morning at 0200 on a contracted "Seaboard and Western" Super Constellation. We felt pretty good about it except it meant we wouldn't have any time to check out the nightlife in California. After a shower and shave, we slipped into comfortable civilian clothes and strolled down to the Officers Club for a couple of drinks and a big steak dinner. The place was packed as we found out there were many aircraft going in and out from the Pacific and officers, high-ranking civilians, and dependents were keeping the club well heeled. That doesn't seem to be the case these days. The drinks, food service, and prices at the Officers Club were very good. Kitch and I found all kinds of friendly people who wanted to drink and tell us about their travels. We were directed not to talk about what we would be doing at Eniwetok, so we avoided saying any more than that we were going to Hawaii.

The two of us were playing "horses" with the dice cup at the bar for our second drinks and for the drinks of two Red Cross girls on their way to the Far East when a voice called Kitch's name. Turning around, I noticed a smiling, stocky man who was dressed in a slightly wrinkled 1505 Khaki uniform shirt and pants. He had no tie on so we knew he had come into the bar from the card room area where they didn't have to wear a tie after 5 PM A tie was required in the main bar after 5 PM and in "civvies," you must also wear a coat. I heard Kitch say his name with the inference of an old buddy, "Willy Field classmate and poker hustler." After a few friendly and exuberant slaps on the back and hand clasps, I was introduced to "Slick McDuggin." It turned out that he and three other pilots, one another classmate of Kitch's, were on their way to pick up some B-26's in the Philippines. They were playing cards in the casual lounge and we excused ourselves from the Red Cross girls and joined the poker game with Slick and his companions. They were leaving on a Flying Tiger DC-6 flight at 8 PM, so we just had time for a few hands and some get-acquainted stories before they had to leave for the passenger terminal. They were going to eat at the flight line cafeteria, as they didn't feel like putting their ties on and then have to rush through the meal at the Officers Club dining room. We walked out the front door and watched them board the special bus. It was sent to the Officers Club prior to each "MATS" aircraft scheduled departure for passengers just as other buses were sent to the NCO Club, the Airmen's Club, and the Transient Quarters.

The two of us drifted back into the club and had a great dinner with shrimp cocktail, filet mignon, salad bar (newly started in California) and good wine. After supper, we drifted back into the bar and decided that after a nightcap we'd try to get a few "Z's" before our long flight to Hawaii.

Our scheduled departure time was 0200, so we left a wake-up call for midnight and then departed to our individual rooms for two short hours of sleep. We planned on sleeping some on the airliner but both of us knew that it was not very easy to get much real rest that way. We were awakened at the appointed hour and showered, dressed, packed our civvies, and climbed into our traveling uniforms—summer shirt and pants. The bus picked us up at 0100 and we checked in with the departure desk at the terminal building. They assigned our seats and when the families and V.I.P.s traveling on official orders were called to board and had gone out to the aircraft, they called for officers traveling on official orders. That was us, and we gladly climbed on board, followed by the enlisted men on orders and then by the people traveling on "space available" status (mostly retired military).

We were pleased to see the crew was well supplied with stewardesses and we were immediately offered coffee when we were seated. I didn't drink coffee at that time but I accepted orange juice in its place. Finally, the doors were closed and the left outboard engine roared to life, followed by the left inboard engine. While we sat there awaiting the other two engines to start, the old "Connie" was shaking and rattling like it was trying to do the Tango. As soon as all four engines were running the old bird seemed to settle down to the normal even vibrations and we started to taxi. We stopped at the end of the runway while the pilots ran up each engine and made their standard pre-take-off checks. Kitch and I were both aware that one engine didn't sound just right when it was undergoing its run-up check and we could both tell that it wasn't going to pass muster when the second and third run-up try didn't sound any better than the first. Our suspicions were soon confirmed by our turn around and taxi back to the terminal area.

The captain announced that there would be a slight delay so the ground maintenance crew could look over a slight problem with one of the engines. It would require that we all disembark back to the gate area where an announcement would be made as to the next scheduled departure time. It was now almost 0300 and by 0400, we were told to go back to the transient quarters and await a call telling us the new departure time. We checked back into the V.O.Q. and had just gotten to sleep when a knock on the door announced a new scheduled take-off time of 0900. I realized that I wasn't going to get any sleep, so I dressed and walked to the Officers Club for breakfast. Kitch soon showed up and as we were waiting for the bus to pick us up, the pilots who had left ahead of us for the Philippines came walking up to the club from the V.O.Q. They were as surprised to see us still there as we were to see them.

Their story was similar to ours except they didn't even board their aircraft before the flight was cancelled. They had a noon take-off scheduled, so once again we said good-bye. This time we were told that our flight had further delays and it would be 1300 before our departure, so we went back to the Officers Club to meet the Philippines group playing poker. About an hour later, they excused themselves from the game, we said our good-byes again, and they left. We didn't board the bus until 1230, and since we had only to walk onto the aircraft when it was ready, that allowed us plenty of time. When we entered the terminal building, who should we see waiting to catch the bus back to the club but McDuggin and his group. Their story was the same and we exchanged good-natured barbs about having Mai Tai's waiting for them when their flight finally got to Hawaii. Their laugh came when we walked into the club at 1500 as we had once again been cancelled. This time I checked with one of the pilots on our aircraft while he was getting food in the terminal snack bar. He told me that they were awaiting a part, which was being shipped from the East Coast, and he was certain it could not arrive before 2000. With that information in hand, we knew we couldn't depart before 2200. It didn't make sense to check back into the V.O.Q., so we returned to the poker game at the club.

Our new, "old friends," greeted us with cheers at having us back. There were more jokes about how we enjoyed the Mai Tai's. We all had another good supper together at the club and they departed at 2100. We had been scheduled once again for a 2300 departure and as they left us they said that if they had a long layover at Hickham Field in Hawaii, they would consider treating us to a Mai Tai. Kitch and I arrived at the terminal at 2230 and whom should we find sitting in the waiting area? Their flight had a confirmed additional "short" delay so we waved to them as we exited towards our waiting "Connie".

This time we made it off the ground but from my view out of the window, it seemed as though we barely skimmed over the hills between Travis AFB and the Berkeley area. As we flew opposite the Bay Bridge it still appeared that we weren't much higher than the tops of the towers passing over the Golden Gate Bridge. Our aircraft flew into the low overcast and I decided that if we were going to stay at that low altitude there would be nothing to hit until we reached the Hawaiian Islands. The old bird struggled for a long time and then my nap was shaken by the sudden change in the steady drum of the engines to a definite increase in noise. In my drowsy state, it took a second or two before I realized that the engineer had just shifted to the superchargers.

The trip was uneventful and Kitch and I slept off and on during the ten-hour flight. We arrived early in the morning but were surprised to find one of the bomber flight engineers there to meet us. We had been told that the bomber task force commander would arrange for rooms at the Reef Hotel for us and have transportation waiting. With all of the delays, we were still only 28 hours late in arriving, so we expected to have rooms waiting, but not transportation. While we waited for our bags, we noticed that McDuggin's flight was arriving in thirty minutes. I picked up my bags and removed a large baritone ukulele that I had vowed I would learn to play during the six-month stay on the island. We bought orchid lei's and when the troops walked into the terminal we delighted the crowd by playing and singing "Aloha Oy" and hanging the flowered rings over the necks of the Philippines bound pilots.

Having had our fun, we headed for Waikiki Beach and our hotel. The desk at the Reef informed us that they had no reservations for us, so I went to the phone and called Chuck Anderson, the Commander of the B-52. It was only 0830 and my call woke him from his much-needed rest. A sleepy voice didn't sound too happy to hear from me but managed to say that he had rooms across the road on the beach side at another hotel. It turned out to be two suites, which were not cheap, but we figured we weren't going to have any place to spend money for the next six months and we were so tired that any place to sleep was welcome. Chuck managed to say that they would be down by the pool at the Reef later in the day.

After a short sleep, I was anxious to find out where we were as far as scheduled time to go to Eniwetok. Kitch and I had our choice of riding down to the island on the B-52 or flying on the regular MATS C-97. We walked over to the swimming pool at the Reef Hotel about 1300 and found a few of the Bomber group and engineers enjoying the condiments such as exotic cocktails and lunch along with the great number of scantily clad women taking in the sun. "Bomber Andy" wasn't there but one of the other officers told me they expected to be there at least ten more days. At the time that sounded great to me and Kitch, but our planned expenses were not as grand as the Bomber groups. Besides, they had taken all of the penthouses and by sharing them with two or four to a suite, they cut expenses for lodging. The suites they had arranged for us were substantially more expensive, so we didn't have the resources to stay the full ten days.

The parties were something to behold as the advanced group had met many local and touring women who were looking for something to do with their evenings. The penthouses, with their large balconies and adjoining porches, offered a great place to throw an open house type party every night. I vividly remember one night when one of the local guests started teaching us how to make sun hats out of palm fronds. Kitch and a few of us began making them and we got our palm fronds by reaching over the balcony rails and grabbing the closest ones and pulling the top of the trees towards the building to a point where we could cut them off with a machete that someone removed from a survival kit.

The hats became such a hit with all of the guests that the supply of fronds ran lower than the demand for hats. It was time for a fighter pilot to take charge of the situation, so I elected myself as project manager and "go-fer" to provide more fronds. We had stripped most of the fronds from the balcony side of just about all of the trees that were reachable from the various balconies and porches. I searched and found a tree that had one reachable frond. Kitch and Tom Sumner, the B-47 test pilot, helped me pull the frond close enough to allow me to step over into the top of the tree.

Yep, that was great planning on my part and was induced by the deadening of one part of my gray cells by those wild Hawaiian rum drinks. (The part that tells you what's not the smart thing to do and doesn't affect that part that tells you there is nothing you can't do.) I assessed the situation and decided that the tree was strong enough to hold me because it was old enough to grow to a height as tall as the fourth floor porch.

The only way we were going to get more fronds to satisfy the hat demand was to cut those from the side away from the hotel, which we couldn't reach without climbing aboard the trees and hacking away. There I was with that large knife in one hand and hanging onto whatever I could grab onto in the top of the palm tree. As soon as it looked like I was in the center to my happy companions, who were holding the tree in towards the porch railing, they joyfully let go, sending the tree and me speeding away from the hotel like a slingshot. I was spread-eagled over the center of the tree with my one arm hugging the saw-toothed base of the palm fronds on the far side of the tree and the machete waving wildly in my other hand. I'm sure that anyone watching from the ground would have thought some Wildman from Borneo was attacking from the trees. About the time the tree reached the end of its first half cycle, I was sure I was going to be flung headlong into the building across the street. I swear that I was looking straight down into the middle of the street below and began to suddenly feel that maybe I should have studied the potential hazards before volunteering for this mission. The trunk of that tall, tall tree looked like a toothpick climbing up from that very small spot next to the sidewalk some four floors below.

As I continued to ride the tree through its several decreasing oscillations, I seriously began to question my judgment and the strength of that long skinny tree trunk. I was also aware that my hand and arm, which were clinging in a death grip on those sharp palm frond bases, were being scratched and were burning.

When the tree finally settled down, I repositioned myself in a sitting posture. I was not comfortable because of the pinecone configuration that forms the top of all palm trees. The only way I could brace my body to hack at the fronds and still hold on to them was to sit on that pinecone, so I ignored the pain and got my balance and leverage in the proper angles and started chopping on my first frond. After cutting it and turning around to hand it to someone on the porch, I became aware that I had attracted a crowd. I didn't want to change my position and couldn't lean far enough towards the railing to have anyone reach it so I wedged my feet in between the ridges in that "pine cone" top. I could hear some laughter at my crazy position but a few sane voices were begging me to get out of the tree. I knew that would probably be easier to say than to do, so I went about cutting more palm fronds, being very careful not to cut that one which was reachable from the porch. After cutting some eight fronds, I carefully re-positioned myself making sure not to look down. I tossed the cut "hat material" over to waiting hands, one at a time.

To my chagrin, when I finished tossing the last one to the porch there was no one who seemed interested in helping me back. Some of the partygoers were enjoying themselves by laughing at my predicament, but finally, Kitch and a couple of other troops came back and began to take an interest in the possibilities of getting me back. I heard someone say they were going to call the fire department to get me down. I didn't like the thought of being helped down like a wayward cat. The people on the porch couldn't reach that one frond that we had used to pull the tree over. Either because of my weight in the tree or perhaps we damaged that frond when they were holding it for me, but whatever the reason, I was in a very poor position to get back.

I decided to take charge as I could see that no one else was as interested in retrieving me. I began rocking back and forth and as the tree came closer to the railing, a couple of people grabbed the single palm frond. I was in the "ready" position and as soon as the tree stopped for an instant, I pushed off with my anchored rear foot. Eager hands reached out and pulled me to safety. The unfair part of the exercise was that every one of those fronds had been used and none was left for me to make a hat of my own. For the next six months, I was not allowed to forget it, as all of those who had made hats were wearing them on Eniwetok. I had plenty of scratches and tears in my pants to remind me for the rest of my Hawaiian stay, especially when I went into the salt water.

With a few other lesser escapades, Kitch and I ran out of money in five days and opted to head on down to the islands on a C-124 (which officially had been banned from carrying passengers). It was another week before the bombers began to straggle in.

ENIWETOK ATOLL

My home for the next six months.

Kitch and I followed Brownie to the officers' mess, which was just a few tables situated in a corner of the main mess hall. After a pretty decent meal, we set out to explore the island and that didn't give us very much exercise or take very long. Just across the street from the mess hall was the "beach" which faced the inside lagoon. The water was a beautiful yellow-green out about a hundred yards off the beach and then sharply turned into a deep blue. The lagoon looked almost as smooth as glass and there were dark patches dotting the light-colored areas pointing out the underwater coral trees, which climbed from the floor forty feet below the surface to just a foot or two below the glassy top. The Holmes and Narver men maintained this small recreational beach, and there were several small 12 and 14-foot sailboats. We noticed that they were chained and locked with no masts or sails.

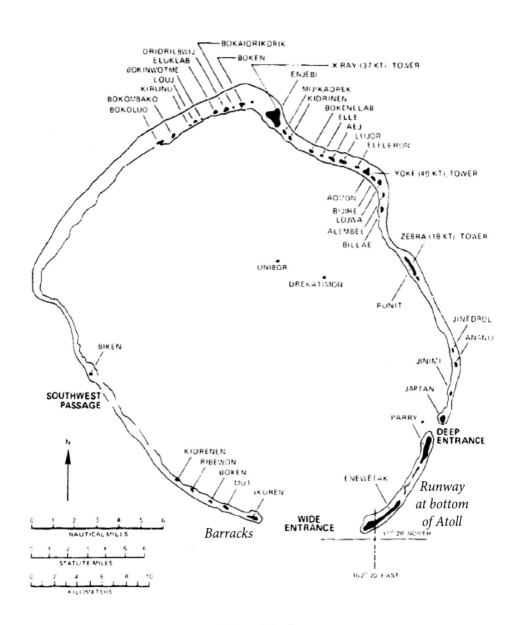

Eniwetok Atoll

I learned a few days later when I tried to check one out to sail around the lagoon that they were no longer available. A few weeks before I arrived, one of the H & N men had taken one in the middle of the night and headed for Hawaii, never to be seen again. It didn't take too many weeks on that isolated rock to understand why he had tried it. (Not that I had ever gotten that drunk or desperate.) At the western end of the atoll was a dumping ground (in the water) for all of the relics left from the war. There were landing craft hulls, tanks, all types of vehicles and armament just lying there rusting in the corrosive saltwater and humid air. This was located just off the end of the runway. All of the landings I made during those five and one-half months and 77 flights from that runway were to the east making all of my approaches over the World War II graveyard.

The sewage dumping pipes ran out into the inlet on that end of the island and the rusting barrier formed a protective bay that attracted the many sharks and other fish. Kitch and I had brought two spear guns over with us. One I had bought and the other he had spent a lot of time making. His was larger and he had bought a much larger spear than mine. He had powered it with several large hospital-acquired bungee tubes. We took the guns down to the sewage dump area and I tried several times to fire mine from the shore but the line wasn't long enough to reach the sharks that were swimming everywhere in that small bay.

Kitch took his mighty weapon and scornfully showed me that the homemade efforts were truly more in keeping with the size needed for these Pacific sharks. He drew a bead on a big one that came into range and I watched in awe as he let the spear fly with deadly accuracy. He had done a masterful job in constructing that gun from laminated hickory and the trigger system from a shotgun. The large spear streaked dead-on through the air and struck the large shark just below his exposed fin. The shark quivered and stopped as if stunned for perhaps a tenth of a second and then to my surprise and Kitch's shock and horror, the shark accelerated away from us at just under the speed of light and so did the spear, the line and the spear gun, which left Kitch's hand before he knew what happened. I will never forget the look on his face; totally unbelieving, as his many hours of labor disappeared out to sea while he stood there, still unable to comprehend what had just happened.

The aircraft carrier had arrived ahead of us with our two F-84F's aboard but we couldn't fly because of grounding flight safety tech orders, which had to be complied with. They couldn't be done until copies of the Technical Order (T.O.) were received, so there was little for Kitch and I to do but settle in to a way of life compatible with our new isolation from the outside world. It took two weeks for my airplane to be readied for its first flight. Kitch's F-84F was an older model and they were able to have his readied a day ahead of mine, as it did not have as many items to be checked.

About a week after we arrived, our bomber troops flew in and among the items carried on board were such needed "toys" as an 18-foot outboard motor boat and a small sunfish sailboat. We had all pitched in and paid for them back at Dayton and they turned out to be a great investment. Also, in the specialty items shipped to me for keeping until the owner arrived, was a scuba breathing regulator and dual air tanks. Lt. Bob Mercer was the Radist Space Positioning Project Engineer and I had spent a lot of time with him at Patrick Air Force Base in Florida while testing the system and that was the reason he sent them in my care. It certainly wasn't because I knew anything about scuba diving. It took a day or two to wangle a deal with the Holms and Narver folks who were in charge of the compressed air equipment, to allow me to fill the tanks. I still don't know whether or not the compressors were equipped with filters for human breathing but as far as I know, none of us suffered from its use.

I didn't realize how dumb we were to scuba dive when none of us had ever had scuba lessons or for that matter knew that there were such things. I was elected, by my own decree of possession being nine-tenths of the law, and out into the lagoon we sailed in our outboard motor boat. I climbed over the side and then worked the cylinders onto my back, put on my facemask, and then put the regulator mouthpiece in my mouth. I slipped under the water but didn't stay under more than a few attempted breaths when I realized that it was "different" from normal breathing. The effort required that I force my intake and then force out my exhale breathing in order to open and close the regulating valves. Not having spent much time in the ocean before, it took a while for me to feel comfortable enough to venture down to any depth. Some of the other crewmembers were harassing me to let them test it, as I seemed to be tentative in my efforts. Aside from Kitch, I wasn't going to let a "bomber puke" outdo me. I didn't know until 10 years later that I was doing a very dumb thing.

In 1966 while working as a civilian astronaut on the Manned Orbiting Laboratory, I helped develop and test an underwater simulation of a zero gravity system. They sent me to Los Angeles County and the University of Southern California to be certified as a scuba diver. That's when I found out how lucky we all were that none of us had any problems with embolisms or the bends. Particularly when Kitch and I were flying our F-84's at high altitudes with our minimal pressurization, and other times after diving with the scuba gear. We were also alone when we left the surface even though the others would follow above on the surface with their snorkeling gear.

The inability for those on the surface to help when the need arrived became crystal clear on one of my first dives. I had mastered the breathing technique and was feeling confident and adventurous. I had my little spear gun and decided to explore one of the big coral trees. I had read enough about the underwater creatures that inhabit the South Pacific and knew that the moray eels were feared by the natives—far more than were the sharks. I also knew that they made their homes in the coral trees. They would hide in a hole in the tree and wait for their prey to pass close enough to them so they could shoot out and grab it, pulling it in against the tree with their three layers of needle sharp teeth. I also had read that they would not let go of anything they locked onto. In order to get free you would have to cut off their head (something I found out later was impossible to do with the diving knives we carried with us).

On this particular exploration, I was following a very large grouper (sea bass) that I guessed weighed 50-60 pounds. I spotted him leisurely swimming outside of the tree and he let me approach him without too much concern about my presence. After all, he was not much smaller than I was and he seemed curious about what kind of creature I was. When I was within six feet of him, he decided he had seen all he needed to see and quickly slid into the safety of the coral tree. These trees are made of large caves, which not only have entrances on the sides but on the tops as well. They vary in circumference and I would guess this one was about 60 to 70 yards around. Looking into the larger entrances you can see deep into the center of the tree and I watched as a large fish retreated into the depth of his safe haven and turned and looked back out to see if I was following him in. The entrance was too small for a man and I wasn't about to get too close to the caves for concern over becoming prey to a large moray.

I was fascinated by all of the beautifully colored fish that inhabited the trees and the killer clams that were encrusted into the tree itself. They would open their iridescent purple mouths to attract the more inquisitive fish to their doom. While I was "standing," about ten feet off from the entrance that the grouper had gone through, something caught my attention and as I turned to look, I thought a submarine was passing behind me. I had no doubt about it not being a submarine and was certain it was the biggest shark I had ever seen, or hope to ever see again that close.

He was probably 20 feet away from me and was slowly passing by, but that eye which was observing me looked to be at least as large as a dinner plate. The louvered gills behind that eye looked to be four feet high and I thought the whole mass of that long thick body would never stop passing by. Finally, the tail disappeared around the tree and I started to move out to head for the boat when I saw that big nose coming back in the other direction. He had noticed me and wanted a closer look. I forgot all about moray eels and backed up against the coral as close as I could and pointed that little spear gun at the other eye that was now staring directly at me with obvious interest. He was no farther away than ten feet this time and I tracked that eye with my gun but hoped there would be no need to test its ability to discourage the monster. I don't think I breathed for the whole indeterminable period that the shark took to pass and circle back around the other side of the tree. I gave him at least a minute and when I didn't see him returning, I headed back to where I had last seen the boat.

I knew that you were not supposed to splash or create a commotion that would lead the shark to think you were wounded or in trouble, but the second I saw the bottom of the boat on the surface about twenty feet above me and a hundred feet away I practiced being a torpedo and headed straight for the refuge. They tell me that I broke the surface of the lagoon much the same as a flying fish does and that my flippers were moving so fast that I walked on the top of the water until I grabbed the side of the boat and almost capsized it climbing aboard. Of course, the other snorkelers had seen the shark heading for me and had retreated to the safety of the boat, wondering whether I would show up. That was as close as I ever want to be to a giant white tiger shark and to this day I don't even like to watch them through the aquarium glass!

On March 26, 1956, my F-84 was ready for a functional test flight to see that all of the systems were working after its long trip across the Pacific Ocean on the deck of a small CVE class aircraft carrier. The aircraft was in good shape and on the next morning, I made my first trip around the course that I would fly so many times in the months to come. My flight plan called for me to take-off to the east and turn right to a heading of west while climbing to 10,000 feet. When I had traveled 10 miles west of the island and still at 10,000 feet, I turned to a heading of 360 degrees north. As I passed a point that was an imaginary line extending across Eniwetok directly through "ground zero," the point on which the bomb was going to be exploded on Bikini, which was 210 miles to the east, I was to turn on my Radist transmit switch. This action turned on all of the Radist magnetic tape machines at all of the tracking stations located on islands hundreds of miles away. I then climbed to a predetermined altitude, which changed for each mission and then I proceeded to the northeast.

Our radar station at Eniwetok followed my progress and gave me heading corrections to keep me on my pre-selected course. At a point, about 60 miles to the northeast of my take-off point, I was vectored on a southeast heading towards Bikini. Shortly thereafter I left the radar control for 6 to 8 minutes until the command ship near Bikini picked me up on their scopes. Radist control also tracked me but on the flights when I was transmitting data to them, they couldn't direct me. Atomic operations control was the main Bikini area control and they were the real mission control radar that monitored all of the aircraft in the test force during the actual "shot." Because of the position of Bikini relative to all of the other islands in the Marshall Group, the rescue and the control vessels were all stationed to the south of the line between Eniwetok and Bikini. All of the other test force aircraft flew their routes to Bikini south of that same line so that they were always within easy range of a rescue ship or aircraft. I never understood why I was sent on that lonely 380 mile run to the target in my single engine fighter, while the multi-engine aircraft all flew on the route where they had the comfort of knowing there were rescue aircraft and ships available to them should the need arise.

Back to my flight pattern—I was on my own, flying a pre-determined heading until Bikini control radar picked me up and gave me my track to point zero. (A position relative to the location of the bomb and my spot in space that I had to occupy at the instant the bomb was exploded). At that point, all of the Radist tracking stations "marked" and stopped receiving information from me. I was then free to find my way back to Eniwetok with the help of radar following. I needed them as the heavily instrumented F-84F I was flying had only an ADF receiver and it was only operational when I was within 15 miles of Eniwetok. Of course, I didn't know this until my first flight away from the island and as I headed home, I had determined that the system was inoperative. Only when I was well within sight of the island and made a few turns did I find that the system was working, but limited in reception range.

On that first flight to Bikini, the weather was beautiful all the way. On my return, I noticed the CVE carrier, which had brought my aircraft across the ocean, and decided I would give them a friendly buzz job.

There are two things that are taught to pilots who fly over water and they are: 1) never fly close to the water unless you have an object on the water to give you a fixed reference as to how high you are above the surface and 2) don't fly close to the water unless you have something on the surface to give you a reference to your height above the surface!

I had this large aircraft carrier and having been on board aircraft carriers before, I knew how huge they were. While I was making my wide descending circle, I planned to come past at a height below the level of the flight deck and then pull up performing a series of rolls as I climbed skyward. I leveled off about a mile behind and below the deck level of the ship and had a hard time comprehending the size of the two helicopters that were sitting on the flight deck. They looked gigantic! It was only when I passed close beside and below the level of the flight deck that I realized the true size of these miniature carriers. The men standing on the deck appeared to be 12 feet tall and the misjudged size of the ship was very clear to me by then.

I hauled back on the stick and pointed skyward performing my series of rolls, happy to be going away from that restless ocean that had almost claimed another victim. Several nights later in the dining hall, I met the captain of the ship and related my surprise at its size. After he complimented me on the splendid buzz job, he said he had to admit that the Navy had never made any passes as low as mine and that the sailors on the deck said they could see water spraying up behind my tailpipe. I naturally refrained from telling him of my mistaken judgment of the CVE's size and thus my altitude above the water. I just told them I was paying my respects to his ship and its crew for bringing my F-84 safely across the Pacific in such good condition.

Following the flight path transmitting run, the Radist stations had to synchronize their tapes so that they could all start at exactly the same instant and provide me with the one tenth of a second accuracy I had to have at "time zero," (the time of bomb detonation). This took a couple of days, so on my next flight I followed the same procedure, except when I passed the point 10 miles west of Eniwetok the Radist station started sending me the signals they had recorded from my system on the previous flight. I had an old type ILS indicator mounted on top of my instrument panel. The two needles were hinged on the top and side of the instrument face, the vertical needle gave me course information, and the horizontal needle gave me progress. The sensitivity of the two systems tightened as I approached closer to time zero. At 10 minutes to go, the progress needle had to be in the center circle. I was trying to keep both of them positioned as close to center as possible. Each of the three dots above and three dots below the circle indicated increments of one minute, changed to 30 seconds. At seven minutes to go they changed to 10 seconds and at 3 minutes to go they changed to 1 second. At 30 seconds before time zero, or time of bomb detonation, they changed to 1/10 of a second.

It is unbelievable that those types of tolerances can actually be flown but I can tell you that it can be done. As I had to prove on each of my seven live missions, any time the needle was more than three dots ahead or behind in progress, I could be in too close for the predictable survivability of the aircraft. When I was ahead of my tenth of a second tolerance, the needle was below the center, so I had to slightly reduce power. I could be too far from the desired position in space to get the maximum data. These tolerances I had to meet were the most demanding and difficult flying I have ever had to perform in my 75 years of active flying. The kicker was that the yield of the experimental hydrogen bombs could not be accurately predicted. I knew that even if my job was done correctly, I could still end up not getting the maximum heat and load heat if the yield was low or I could get too much heat and load if the yield was higher than predicted.

The latter happened to me on my seventh shot and ended my participation in the project. After having to remain silent about this whole project for 62 years, as we were directed to do, not even discussing it with our wives, I felt that my memory of the tolerances of the system might be inaccurate. I dug out a small diary I had written and kept well-hidden for all of these years. My one tenth of a second desired accuracy was there in writing in my notes.

I was looking forward to my first encounter with the "bomb" with mixed interest and trepidation. I knew that I was to be placed closer than any of the other aircraft had ever been in any of the other tests flown by manned aircraft. I was going to have to fly that unstable fighter on instruments for 40 to 50 minutes to time tolerances I was sure couldn't be done. The Radist system had only worked properly on a few of the test flights that Kitch and I flew down at Patrick Air Force Base and failure rates were very high, making confidence level very low. To add to that, the bombs were experimental, which meant that the scientists' "guesstimated" yield of the weapons were just that!

If that weren't enough to keep me awake at night, there was the fact that I was flying over two hundred and eighty miles of open ocean before reaching Bikini with hardly any chance of being rescued in the event anything happened to my single engine aircraft along that route. If I suffered engine failure before or at the time of the explosion, which was one of the tests being conducted (to see what effect was caused by the high overpressures of the bomb's shock wave as it impacted the tailpipe of the engine) there was no chance of rescue as I would be in the heavy radiation and fallout zone.

No one knew whether the high pressure of the shock wave would be strong enough to create a backpressure on the turbine wheel and cause the engine to flame-out or possibly come "unglued." That was only one of the possibilities that could occur as the other tests on my research vehicle were to determine how much structural loading the airframe could withstand in dynamic flight; what effect would the extreme heat from the hydrogen bomb have on the various thicknesses of metal on the aircraft skin or Plexiglas canopy; and what effect would it have on the pilot's ability to survive and function to control the aircraft providing the aircraft continued to operate after the heat and shock wave hit!

Prior to coming to the island, the real dangers and risks were never discussed in much detail. However, they were, once we were in place. My particular exposure was explained to me in a private briefing by some nuclear scientists from Sandia, the Air Force facility where nuclear scientists were assigned. All of the test aircraft had more than their share of risk involved in flying in these bomb tests. Mine was a little more unique as I had to be placed closer than any of the other aircraft because my F-84F was the strongest plane structurally.

During the manufacturers structural integrity testing of all aircraft, they conducted static loads tests on the aircraft by placing sand (or lead) bags on the wings and stabilator until they failed and computed what they called "ultimate structural failure g load." They performed the same test on the vertical tail and rudder by turning the aircraft on its side on the test stand. For measuring negative structural limit load factor data they mounted the airframe upside down and performed the same test on the bottom of the wings and tail (more modern methods put them in specially designed jigs that bend and vibrate the airframe to measure the possible life cycle of the aircraft). This data was always taken before the aircraft was manufactured and then we "test pilots" verified its validity by flying and pulling 80% of those limit loads in flight. If the airframe didn't fail or crack at the 80% point of the limit load factor, the structural integrity of the aircraft was proven.

Now that combat aircraft were going to have to have the capability of delivering nuclear weapons, someone (probably a pilot) decided that when they dropped the bomb with the high kiloton, and now hydrogen mega-ton yields, it would be nice to know whether or not they had to lose every aircraft sent on those missions by being destroyed by the bomb that was dropped. It was widely believed by the pilots who stood on nuclear alert all around the world that if they had to drop their bombs, particularly fighter aircraft, they could possibly survive.

Evans and Kitchens (in flight suits) with support engineers.

BACK ON THE ISLAND

I was given more detailed information as to what kind of data was needed from my aircraft. The one element that was never emphasized was the amount of radiation I would be subjected to by being so much closer to the bomb's explosion than anyone had been before or has been since! (Obviously, I survived and there can't be the suspense for the reader that a fiction novelist could build up for you at this point in the story. If I can give some faint idea as to what you would experience in one of these blasts, I think it will be worth your while to keep reading.) The briefings we had prior to leaving Dayton were very specific as to the amount of radiation each of us would be allowed to be exposed to during the six-month period. I'm not exactly certain now what the actual allowable dosage was, but I believe it was about 800 millirem for that period of time. I only know that I had 1,000 on my visual radiometer pen after my first live mission. (They only registered as high as 1,000)

I was ready to leave for home, but the flight surgeon said that they were ultra-conservative numbers and that I would not be sent home. (He proved to be consistently unresponsive to my concerns about the high levels of radiation that I was being exposed to and I was ordered to continue to fly the missions, probably because there was no one else trained to do it.)

As the days dragged on towards the first live shot, code name "Lacrosse," my thoughts were of facing the true test of man and machine versus the bomb. I mixed discovery of the underwater life of the South Seas with every day work routines. I flew almost every day on practice missions validating the Radist reliability and giving training in the use of the system to all of the operators at the Radist sites and of course to me. In the time I was not involved with briefing, flying, and de-briefing, we played softball, chess, and wrote letters home. One of the standards each night after supper was to attend the movies.

Our theater was a group of portable stands such as they used for school athletic events and a large movie screen mounted on the edge of the shore. There was no problem with light interfering, as there were no lights coming from the lagoon. It was similar to the drive-in movies without the cars or the girls. We would buy popcorn, take our rain ponchos, and visit the outside world up there on that screen for 2 to 4 hours (depending on whether or not it was a double feature). When it rained, which it often did, we just pulled the poncho over our heads and covered the popcorn bag and tried to see the show through the down pouring stream and run-off from the poncho. It didn't seem to matter just how bad the movie was. Most of us sat through them to the end.

One night, while sitting through a second feature with a

very heavy downpour, the sky suddenly erupted with a bright orange light that was accompanied by a rumbling sound. The light grew in intensity and then slowly turned to a steady glow. You can imagine the first thought that came into the minds of most of us sitting in the heart of a nuclear test area and knowing that the devices were being assembled on the adjacent island to us on the atoll only a mile or two away. It was only a minute or two until I could tell it was on the west end of the island away from the assembly island. There was nothing there but runway, so it was probably an aircraft.

We had supply, mail and transports arriving every few days and it appeared one of them had crashed on the end of the runway. Several of us from my group went to our jeep and drove down to the scene of confusion. There, outlined by the fire against the black heavy rainy night sky, was the top half of a two-story C-124. "Our mail plane!" I don't think I heard anybody ask if the crew had gotten out but there was a lot of talk about getting to the mailbags and some very ugly comments about what should be done with the stupid pilot who was flying the machine, assuming he got out of the aircraft safely.

All the crew did, but a lot of the mail didn't, and they were the most unpopular people on the island until they could be transported away back to civilization. The burned hulk had to be cleared from the runway as it blocked the approach end and no aircraft could land until it was removed. In the case of all test aircraft, we had to stand-down for two days until the wreck could be pushed far enough off to the side to allow a clear take-off and landing path. We had to modify our taxi route to taxi down the runway for the last 1,000 feet, and then turn around on the runway to start our take-off roll. That was no problem for Kitch and for me as we had such short wingspans on our aircraft, but the B-52 and B-47 had to work at getting in position.

All of our actual shot missions were flown in darkness until just after the bomb was exploded. That was a requirement of the people who measured the yield of the weapon, which was done by measuring the light intensity. Any additional light from the dawning sky would affect the validity of the data. It was absolutely necessary that it be completely dark at time zero, but desirable that the daylight occurred as soon after as practical. That meant the larger aircraft departed Eniwetok as early as 3 to 4 hours before daylight. They had sufficient fuel, whereas Kitch and I had no extra fuel whatsoever. We were violating Air Force regulations on every flight as we never had sufficient reserve fuel on any mission and never had an alternate airfield we could reach.

The whole month of April was spent working with Radist and "MSQ" radar control. (We called it Miss Que, the Eniwetok precision radar control for the shots that were set off at our atoll.) On the 12th, I was just departing to the north after initiating the Radist system and was climbing on my northeast heading. I was at about 18,000 feet and just past the northern end of the atoll when I apparently flew through a cloud. (I was under my lightproof hood and couldn't tell that clouds were there until after the event). Suddenly my engine began a violent vibration accompanied by a fire warning light and high tailpipe temperature reading. I shut down the engine, pulled the hood open while turning back towards the airbase some 25 miles behind me. At first I was inside a cloud but quickly cleared from the opaque condition to find that the lagoon was below me. I knew I was not going to try a dead stick landing on that short runway and was only looking for an ideal place for me to land after ejecting from the plane.

I knew I wanted to be inside the lagoon. Checking the wind, I felt that I had to make certain that the aircraft didn't crash on any land area. The engine was still shaking the aircraft but the rotation RPM was high enough to maintain hydraulic pressure for the flight controls. The sky was partially covered by puffy cumulus clouds and one was sitting over the runway. The visibility was excellent and the only thing keeping me from following my planned ejection route was one big cloud. I had decided to fly above the active runway and turn towards the lagoon center and eject at about 1,000 feet after trimming the nose down so that the aircraft would dive into the lagoon as soon as I released the stick. That meant I would have to make a very quick ejection sequencing after letting go of the control stick—but first I had to get down below the clouds. I had mixed emotions about having to terminate my participation in the tests and having to eject out of the aircraft. On the other hand, it would mean I could leave this very unpleasant way of life.

Requesting the tower to notify Air-Sea\Rescue that I would be ejecting out over the lagoon, I guessed that I was in a good position to start a 180-degree turn descending into the cloud. After I broke out, I was at 3,500 feet altitude and 45 degrees off the runway heading. Now I am pretty good at determining my glide path and for the first time in this emergency I felt I could save the aircraft. I told the tower I was going to try to land the plane and by lowering the landing gear at the exact right moment I thought I could make it to the runway. Once I made the decision to try to make the runway I was committed with no chance of ejecting if I misjudged my approach. It worked out and I touched down about 1,000 feet down the strip. I coasted off the runway and into my parking area just as though I had made a normal landing with engine power. In fact, it was so uneventful (and also an indication of the attitudes of the people stationed in this out-of-the way base) the flight safety officer was surprised to hear about it two weeks later when I was talking to him at the club.

The engine had thrown a number of turbine buckets through the side of the instrumented tailpipe and through the fuselage. The airframe could be repaired locally but the tailpipe had to be sent to Hickham Air Force Base in Honolulu for repair and re-instrumentation. Any type of logic would dictate that if the tailpipe had to be accompanied by an officer, then I would certainly be the one to escort it. I had saved the aircraft and therefore a very important part of the overall aircraft test program. As long as the tailpipe was being repaired, I had no productive function on the island. Our Test Group Commander, Col. Cobb, sent a bomber pilot whose aircraft was in commission, to accompany my aircraft's tailpipe and I sat there on "The Rock" growing more disgusted and frustrated than ever.

On the 21st of April, my aircraft was back in service with a new-instrumented engine and repaired tailpipe. I went back to work trying to get the Radist System to operate properly. We had all types of failures with the system and those of us who were using it had very low confidence in it, particularly with my tight tolerances. The original F101A that was to participate in the program was damaged beyond repair at Wright-Patterson when the reluctant scheduled pilot for the testing crashed the plane and hurt his back. Major John Apple replaced the injured pilot and a newly instrumented F101A was shipped to Eniwetok for him to fly.

After John arrived on the atoll I received a letter from a friend at flight test operations at Wright-Patterson informing me that the original pilot's back pains must have healed in a hurry as the "patient" was playing Ping-Pong and back on flying status. (This fellow also made General later in his career!)

"During the last seven seconds, I had six sequences of switch position activations and then the last two items were to pull down my black eye shield goggles and place my left hand over them. I thought this was over-kill since I knew that the sealed cockpit hood kept all light out of the cockpit. Boy, was I wrong!"

THE FIRST LIVE MISSION

My mind drifted back to awakening with a start. In a cold sweat, there was not a sound except for the constant pounding of the heavy surf against the coral reef, which had been my home for three months. I strained my ears for some sound of activity from the bomber crews but there was no sound that I could distinguish as being preparation for the scheduled live mission. If they had been told that the shot had been cancelled for today it would mean the tenth delay for this shot. We were all getting jumpy about psyching ourselves up to stick our heads in the lion's mouth. It is like sitting on a powder keg and the only way to get off was for it to explode. You have lit the fuse five times and the fuse or match has gone out so you have to replace the fuse and start all over.

Here I am sitting on the keg with the fuse lit and waiting for some sign that the show is still on. The bomber crews are scheduled to get up at 0130 and head for breakfast. Their take-off times are early enough for them to get to their respective holding areas where the navigators can nail down their wind drift and make several dry runs before the live run. This was no problem since they had plenty of fuel and therefore they were off the ground between 0330 and 0430. Why aren't they getting up? Could the mission have been scrubbed? God, I hope not again! It may not be the nicest way to spend the morning, but that's why I'm here. I am much happier when I can feel the self-satisfaction of doing my job and my job can't be done unless the bomb is detonated.

I lay there for about 20 minutes half-awake when suddenly an alarm clock sounds off down the hall followed by several more. The shuffling of feet, muffled voices, and the roar of the jeeps and weapons carrier is music to my ears. In minutes, I drop back off to relaxed sleep and the next thing I hear is John shaking me and saying it is 0300. Time to get going!

The rain was falling in irregular waves of downpour as Major John Apple, Kitch and I ran from our tin barracks to the open jeep that would take us to breakfast. At the mess hall, we stood in line waiting for our steak and eggs. Not big steaks but more of a token gesture for those of us who are about to step into the "unknown" once more. We are aware of the looks and comments from some of the people that are not getting steaks but we also know that they don't really begrudge us this small luxury, as none of them would trade places with any one of us on this morning. We pass time with small talk during breakfast and are certain that this mission will be scrubbed because of the heavy rain. Most of the large aircraft have already taken off for Bikini so it is apparent that the weather over Bikini is better than it is here.

As the conversation grows slack, we each draw back into our own special thoughts before we tumble into the frenzy of last minute briefings.

The "perk" the test crews were given was to have steak and eggs for breakfast on our live mission day. Sort of a "last breakfast" we halfway joked. It became a status symbol that we all jealously resented when it was served to the non-flying members of the test team. The B-52 and B-47 troops would get up at 0130 and go to the breakfast and then they would come back, get their mission items, and head for their machines. About the time they came back from breakfast, the B-66, A-3D, and B-57 crews would get up and head to the mess hall. While they were eating, the first aircraft would start their engines, taxi past our building within 150 feet and then take-off, passing about 250 feet from our open sided barracks.

The B-52's eight powerful jet engines would act as John's, Kitch's and my alarm clock if we had managed to sleep past the other commotion. It would be our turn to head for steak and eggs. When we returned to the barracks there was no one left to wake up so we would depart for our briefing and then to the aircraft. We had joint mission briefings the evening before each "shot" and last minute weather and bomb status briefing just before take-off. Our project officer, Captain Mitchell, and test engineers Lt.'s Stoltz and Sabutello (Sabu) usually picked up the latest shot schedules and status and gave them to us as we checked the weather ourselves.

Back at breakfast we were each quietly eating and inwardly planning the day's options in case the mission was "hot" and possibilities of limited options should something happen to our mighty steeds as a result of the bomb. We were shaken from our thoughts by the voices of Mitchell, Stoltz and Sabu coming into our area from the regular dining area. From the light tone of their laughter and conversation, we were certain the mission was still on. Kitch and I bolted down the rest of our meal and headed for the rain-drenched jeep while leaving John to wait for his engineer to arrive.

The rain was so heavy that we headed directly to Test Operations where Col. Samuels, the task force "7" commander, gave us some words of encouragement and the weather officer told us that the Bikini weather looked good but the Eniwetok rain and low clouds should remain through the scheduled landing period. That does nothing to improve my high-strung anticipation of the challenges of the morning for Kitch and me. After stopping at the project building to get the latest Radist status update and pick up our flight gear, we separated into two groups to discuss final flight and data plans. Kitch and I fly similar aircraft but our missions are completely different as to the type of data we are gathering and flight paths we are flying. It mostly allows the engineer and maintenance people to feel a part of what is going to happen with their aircraft and the instrumentation once we take off from the island.

I have been through these briefings and practice runs so many times that I don't need to be told anything except the status of the aircraft and systems. The parking area for our two F-84's was well lit and the engineering and instrumentation people were there, finishing their preflight checks along with the Radist technician.

My aircraft had strain gauges and thermalcouples installed throughout the complete airframe. The engine and tailpipe had special instrumentation installed when they were being manufactured for this project. Our parachute, oxygen mask, and helmet were stored in an air-conditioned trailer beside the aircraft and I read the maintenance section of the aircraft's logbook while my crew chief was describing any work that had been done on the machine since my last flight. From there I walked out into the heavy deluge with a poncho covering my head while John Boughman and his assistant crew chief, John Climer, helped by holding each side to keep as much rain off of me, my parachute, and knee-board as possible. I ducked under the wing and pointed my flashlight at the landing gear well and down the bottom of the wing and fuselage, which was really only a formality. I had complete confidence in the thoroughness of the ground crew and this exercise gave me a chance to get out of the direct downpour that was falling and blowing around me. After giving the thumbs-up, I made a quick exit from under the wing and climbed up the ladder as John opened my canopy.

The F-84F has a canopy that opens by moving upward and slightly aft on counter balance arms, which gives some protection from above when it is raining, as it was this morning. While John hurriedly pulled my shoulder straps from behind me to where I could reach them, I waved him away and closed the canopy down as far as it would go with the ladder hooks still in place over the cockpit rail. This allowed John to get back on the ramp, pull his poncho over his head like a tent, and wait for me to pre-flight the cockpit and give the start signal (holding one finger in the air and rotating it in a circular motion).

After strapping into my noble steed, and checking all of the regular aircraft and engine switches for proper pre-starting positions, I went through a detailed instrumentation and

Radist checklist. My final check before starting the engine was with the tower for take-off instructions and test clock "time" hack (synchronize).

My start engine time was determined by the latest winds aloft at my altitude for each mission. I had to be exactly on time and my pre-cut Radist tape depended on my crossing that start point at exactly the right minute. I gave myself an extra few minutes to allow for any delays on the ground caused by an unscheduled landing of one of the other test aircraft or a number of unexpected things that could happen when operating from the only single runway for hundreds of miles.

The difficulty in crossing the starting point ahead or behind was that the Radist progress indication, even though it presented a plus or minus 4 minutes on the initial progress scale (each dot being 1 minute above and below the center circle) did not show whether or not you were on the first or fifth 4-minute error. In other words, I could be six minutes ahead or behind and the only way I could tell which it was would be from the Radist master station controller telling me. He was only able to do that on the final 10 minutes of my run.

I usually taxied out with my canopy open except when it was raining, like this morning, and it was that way about 20% of the flights. After the engine started and all systems were "Go" I signaled John and raised the canopy just enough for him to lift the ladder hooks over the rail and away from the aircraft. Then I closed and locked it. On these rainy mornings it was hard to see immediately after taxiing out of the lighted area, as it was pitch black and the blue taxiway lights were hard to see at first. I could probably have taxied out to the west end of the runway blindfolded by this time, and with the rain streaked windshield giving me double and triple images of the taxiway and runway lights, it was a good thing that I knew the airfield so well.

At the end of the runway, I lined up with the runway lights and checked my gyro compass to see that it checked with a 090 degree (east) heading and checked all of the flight instruments. I was particularly careful to assure myself that the attitude instrument was level because as soon as I pulled the nose wheel off the ground it became my primary indication of my attitude (my reference to my aircraft's position with respect to the horizon). There were no outside visual references with the black sea and sky in front of me.

On this morning, I had to start the first hundred feet or so with my eyes glued to the gyro compass because of the complete obscuration of the forward visibility as I started to roll. At 40 to 50 mph the raindrops seemed to form a solid coating, somewhat distorted, but making it possible for me to see the runway lights.

As the amber lights indicated the last 1,000 feet of remaining runway had passed, I eased back on the control stick and the reluctant F-84 separated itself from the water laden asphalt surface and we were airborne just as the green end of the runway lights passed under my nose. I held the little airplane on the attitude indicator 15 degrees above the horizon and waited for a positive indication of climb rate on my vertical speed instrument and altimeter. When I passed a plus 50 feet, I retracted the landing gear and flaps and continued holding the 15 degrees of climb angle until I reached 500 feet. At that point, I allowed the aircraft to accelerate out to best climb speed and upon reaching it, I started my right hand climbing

180-degree turn to a heading of 270 degrees. I carefully monitored all of the engine instruments on run-up before releasing the brakes for take-off roll and now I re-checked them very carefully. If I had an indication of a problem, I was in position to return to the runway. Once I started on my 480-mile flight there was no place for me to land except in the very inhospitable ocean.

After I crossed my base line and proceeded on the first leg of my journey, I pulled the hood forward and snapped it in place around the instrument panel. This took some effort, so I scheduled it during the least time-consuming portion of my flight. After checking in with mission control, I switched to MSQ control for them to control me by radar.

My workload was extremely demanding during the period from when I turned to the final run heading towards Bikini and the point just after the bombs shock wave hit the aircraft. The heavy hood was made from three layers of laminated aluminum and asbestos cloth. I could slide it along the bottom of the canopy frame on specially constructed rollers. To test it I sat in the cockpit at noon on a bright, sunny day for one hour and could not see one thing inside the cockpit during any of that time. It takes 45 minutes for your eyes to completely adapt to the dark so I was convinced that the hood was as perfectly sealed from outside light as possible. (That makes the incredible occurrence when the bomb exploded even more awesome.) I was seldom off more than 1 minute on my base line starting point on any of the actual live missions (except for one) so I did not have to catch up with the needle past the time frame indicated on the gauge, and flying it was never a problem when in the "4 minute" mode.

The First Live Mission

I flew the same path that my "Radist transmitting" flight sent to the tracking stations on all subsequent flights for each individual shot. The challenge to me was that the winds were never the same on the days that I cut the tape, tramsmitting the signals of my flight path to all the Radist stations for recording. The Radist stations would in turn would transmit the data back to me on all subsequent missions. In other words, when I cut the first mission tape I was at 18,000 feet altitude and the winds varied from 25 to 40 knots from an initial direction of 240 degrees to 360 degrees, enroute to Bikini.

In order to hold a constant heading and power setting, the winds would have had to be exactly the same velocity and direction throughout each of my practice and actual mission flights. This, of course, was an impossibility, and required that I constantly chase the track and progress needles. If I switched to the less sensitive mode, it would not be hard to make these corrections. But I was in the mode where the dots represented 10 seconds and then would have to switch to the next more sensitive mode when each dot represented one second and finally the last mode when each dot was one tenth of a second. This required a real flying effort to keep the needles centered. Keep in mind all of this was being done under the hood in an unstable aircraft where you couldn't take your eyes off the flight instruments for more than a couple of seconds at any time.

The flying effort was enough to occupy most of my thoughts and I believe some psychologists must have given their input in the sequencing of the instrumentation switch activations during the last part of the run before time "Zero." During the last seven seconds, I had six sequences of switch position activations and then the last two items were to pull down my black eye shield goggles and place my left hand over them. I thought this was over-kill since I knew that the sealed cockpit hood kept all light out of the cockpit. Boy, was I wrong!

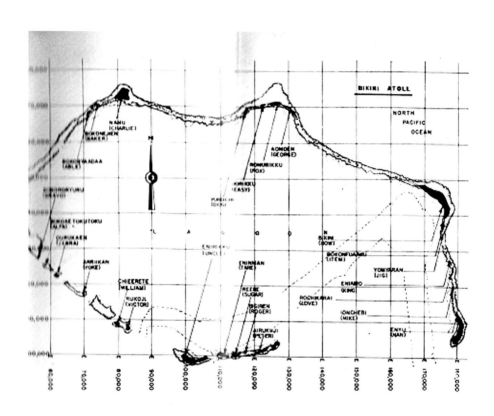

Bikini Atoll with positions of test bomb shots.

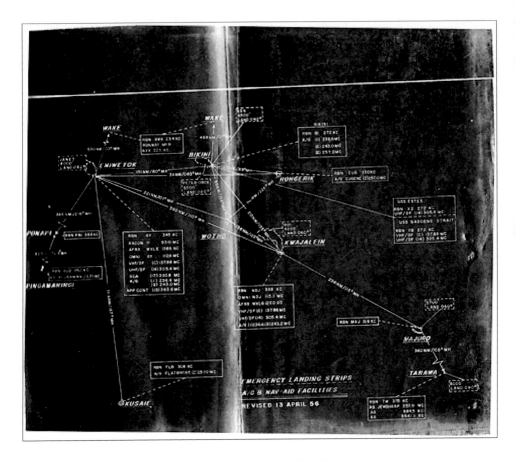

Chart of Emergency Landing Strips

The other pilots could use any of these. Kitchens and I, because of our fuel load, could only use our home base, Eniwetok.

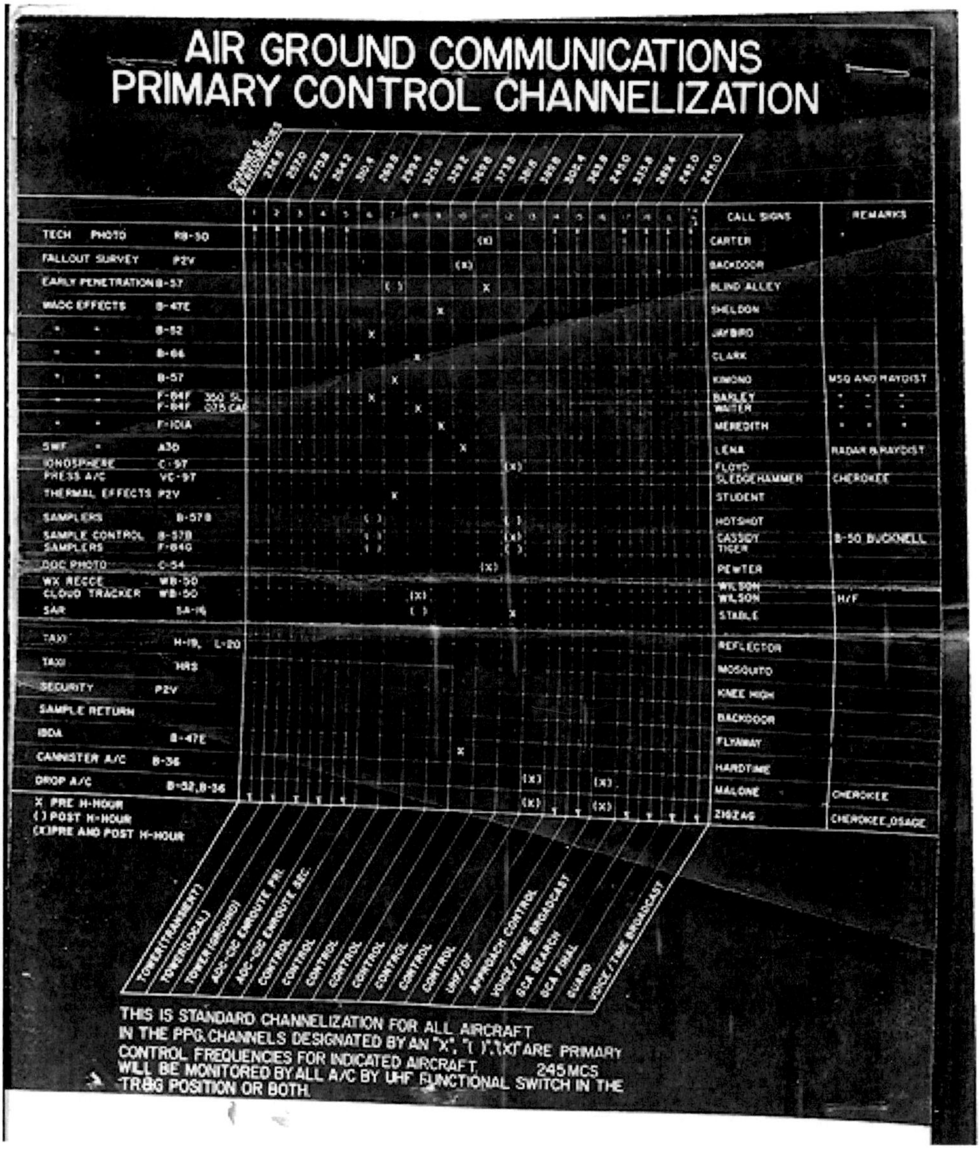

Frequencies of necessary contacts during my test flights.

"As the countdown for the explosion reached "One," I locked my hand on the stick to keep the aircraft in the straight and level position and covered my eyes (goggles) with the other hand.

I had no doubt in my mind that the bomb had detonated as the brilliant light penetrated the cockpit. My gloved hand and black goggles were so white that it hurt my eyes."

THE BOMB'S FIRST LIGHT

On this first live mission, my Radist kept dropping out so we decided to use the MSQ radar voice commands for the final run to the target. I was somewhat concerned about their ability to put me in position within the tolerances I needed. The controller's voice was comforting to hear, but I think he was almost as concerned about putting me over the target on time as I was. He gave me changes of airspeed and headings, which kept me busy. We both knew I had to stabilize on an airspeed altitude and heading at time zero and the aim time was within one tenth of a second. The controller's voice appeared to become more tense as he gave me speed and heading changes to inform me that I was cleared to drop my external tank (a 230-gallon tank under my left wing). It was pretty lonesome up there all by myself, but I wouldn't have it any other way. When you have a few seconds to think about something besides those dials and gauges that keep you aware of your aircraft's attitude, altitude, heading and airspeed, you start to think of those people who are worrying about whether they have computed the position correctly to give you a chance of survival and of the controller who is guiding you to that spot. All of those support people who are pulling for me to come back safely make me decide I would rather be just where I am!

My position is "12½ seconds behind and 15 minutes to go." Then I am "1/2 second ahead and 20 seconds to go."Final count: "5-4-3-2-1-Wow!!" I was given the number of seconds it should take the shock wave to hit my aircraft. If it arrived ahead of schedule it meant the bomb was above its predicted yield and if it arrived late, it was lower than predicted. I wanted it to arrive at least on time. If the bomb was below yield, my data would not be as useful. After making all of the effort on my part to position the aircraft as perfectly as I could, I wanted to give the engineers the data they were looking for. I wasn't disappointed on this shot as it arrived one and one-half seconds early. All of the pre-briefings by pilots from our fighter section indicated that the aircraft would get a "pretty good bump." Had anyone ever been placed in as close a position as I was, I am certain that they would have been more descriptive than they were.

As the countdown for the explosion reached "One," I locked my hand on the stick to keep the aircraft in the straight and level position and covered my eyes (goggles) with the other hand.

I had no doubt in my mind that the bomb had detonated as the brilliant light penetrated the cockpit. My gloved hand and black goggles were so white that it hurt my eyes.

It took two or three seconds before that whitest of all white lights I had ever seen began to fade, but I could still see the bone structure of my hand. Finally, it faded enough for me to take my hand away and start to remove my goggles. The first interest in my mind was to see what had happened to the attitude of the aircraft while I was blinded. The data for shock wave effect was next and I had to be careful to keep the airspeed, altitude, heading, and attitude unchanged until the blast hit me.

As I waited and kept the machine on track I played back what I had just experienced in my mind and had a hard time convincing myself as to what I knew had happened. When I pushed the goggles up from my eyes, the light in the cockpit was still of eye-aching intensity. It rapidly diminished but as it faded, the ultra-violet rays outlined the structural ribs in the airframe the way the sun's rays shine through a broken cloud deck. The other unbelievable thing I wouldn't admit to seeing until the second shot (live mission) I flew in, was that I was certain that I could see the complete bone structure of my hand through the goggles and my closed eyes! Then it hit. It hit with a force, which felt like the impact of crashing into the runway! It took several seconds for the instrument panel and my eyes to allow me to focus after the shock wave from the powerful bombs explosive force impacted the F-84 and on me! Immediately I checked my "g" meter and could see that they were at the maximum recordable levels, which were +22 and -6 g's respectively. (I expect the instrument data recorder had the actual loads but the folks who recorded all the "Effects" data would not release that information to me—as if I was going to tell anyone!)

I have tried to explain to others just what it felt like but

I don't think I have ever been able to adequately put it into words. I was seated on an overwater survival pack, which included a one-man life raft. On top of this molded fiberglass seat was a three-inch thick solidly padded cushion. The shock wave arrived with a teeth-jarring, backbone-compressing hit that caused my eyes to lose their focus for a couple of seconds. It took the instrument panel another few seconds to stop vibrating enough for me to read the attitude indicator to tell me whether the aircraft was still flying upright. I likened it to what I imagined it would feel like if you were seated in a hard-bottomed chair and someone swung a large sledgehammer on an arc from above your head around to hit the bottom of the chair on the upward swing with all of its energy gained throughout the arc. It hurt, and each one that hit me never felt any less powerful than that first one. That was proven on the last shot I participated in where the shock wave was so powerful that—Ah, ah—that comes later.

After the shock wave hit the aircraft and as soon as I could do so, I pulled back the hood and looked at one of the most awesome sights you will ever see. The fireball was always well above me and yet not very far away and was still glowing white, orange and red while it climbed rapidly heavenward, boiling as it went. Below, it left 10 to 15 ultra-violet expanding disks that looked like cirrus clouds but were much too low to be ice clouds. There was nothing but an unbelievable releasing of energy in everything that was associated with the explosion. The fireball and the "stem" of the mushroom cloud still produced enough light to make it easy for me to fly visually. The dim light of the dawning sky on the horizon made it so that I did not have to fly on instruments for the 230-mile trip back to Eniwetok.

During the preparation flights for the first shot, code named Lacrosse, the Radist systems gave us so much trouble that we had to use radar controllers from the test radar MSQ for positioning. I was the only one that there was concern about as my time limitation at time "zero" was so close that we weren't sure they could safely place me at the right spot at the exact right time. They proved to me their ability to do the job with the 0.8 seconds on the actual run, which was much better than they had done on any of the practice runs! This gave me almost perfect position for data. On the return trip to home base, I had to sweat out fuel and weather.

There was also concern that if heat or shock damage occurred to my UHF communications radio I would have no voice guidance back to home plate. Thankfully on this flight, the radio continued to work. I talked to mission control and was controlled back over Eniwetok with a perfect hand-off to "GCA" and a "no sweat" landing with very little fuel remaining. I never did know whether the automatic direction finding radio was working until I was within 15 miles of Eniwetok. When the weather was good at Eniwetok, there was no problem seeing it from the air but as there were always some clouds producing shadows on the water larger than the island, I could likely miss it if I was more than 15 miles off course. Fortunately, I managed to return safely on all of my 77 flights.

After landing, I had to taxi into a decontamination area where men in protective suits and helmets surrounded the aircraft. While I remained inside the cockpit, they washed the aircraft down with high-powered spray guns and then someone would check the outside surfaces with a radiation (Geiger) counter. (One thing on this mission that was certain to me was that if water washed off any contamination from the aircraft it was squeaky clean as I flew through some very heavy rain on my return trip and letdown). Only after this exercise was I allowed to climb out of the aircraft. Any radiation that the plane's skin had absorbed would certainly come into the cockpit through my pressurization system, so they were not trying to protect me, but were concerned about exposing the ground personnel who might have to work on the aircraft.

I taxied back to my parking area, climbed out of the bird wearing only the lightweight summer flight suit. I deposited my flight gear at the personal equipment shack, and walked to the debriefing. I had the opportunity to check my radiometer pencil on the way and on the first mission found that it read above the limits for a six-month period! I was ready to head for Wright-Patterson on the next flight out, as I had a good position and should have gotten maximum data from the shot. I was as familiar with the heat and shock effects of a nuclear bomb as I ever wanted to get. Unfortunately, that was not to be. The flight surgeon who had to act on the radiation dosage told me that the experts were wrong and that I could sustain more dosage than they told me I could.

Gil Rob Wilson wrote an "Ode to a Test Pilot" in which he describes the dives and pulling of maximum "g's" and all of the things a test pilot does to test a new design of an airplane. At the end of the poem, he says: "After you land your brake goes out and you taxi into a ditch—and you don't get paid for the son-of-a-bitch." Well, that's just how I felt the next morning at our debriefing when I was told that the instrumentation had failed and I got "no data." All I could see was that this was going to keep us on the island for an extra "shot." One more mission than I was scheduled to be in and more time on "The Rock."

Evans and Kitchens being congratulated by Republic and Allison tech reps following the first live mission.

"...I felt convinced that the shot was going to "fire." 5-4-2-camera switch "on" -2-goggle "down" 1 "0." Hands over my eyes with a last-minute glance at the attitude indicator to be sure I was flying straight and level. Then it came again. The brilliant white flash of light that was really painful to my eyes and then without trying, I could see all of the bones in my hand. I was closing my eyes as hard as I could but it didn't help."

THE BEAT GOES ON

The day's activities really picked up as everything was being readied for the big "dog and pony show" with the live airdrop of a hydrogen bomb from a B-52. This was big-time publicity and very political. Distinguished Allied and U.S. V.I.P.'s, senators, congressmen, and lots of the press were on hand. Our little island was overrun and our limited resources were strained to the limit. Part of the mess hall was roped off for the visitors and the food we were given was inferior to that served to those "guests." Most stayed for only a day or so after arriving by air and awaiting transportation to the V.I.P. observation ships. The drop was scheduled for the morning of 11 May and was code named "Cherokee."

My diary reads as follows:

Mon: D-3 May 7: *Logged 4 hours and 25 minutes. Radist unsuccessful. Have to log less time than I actually fly so that* aircraft won't have to go into inspection before shot date. I had to make 2 GCA's due to bad weather.

Tues: D-2 May 8: 3 hours and 25. Had to get up at 0430 for 2 unsuccessful Radist runs. Flew air show for visiting V.I.P.s. Kitch had picture taken with wheels but had aircraft trouble so I flew on wing of B-57 with John Apple on the other wing in his F-101A. Partygoers kept me awake until 0130 so not much sleep today.

Wed: D-2 May 9: 1 hour (logged). Radist system still unsuccessful in progress mode. It looks as though mission will have to be flown without progress indicator and will have to use voice control again. The Radist voice controller will have more lag than MSQ but that will be all that will be available on this mission. Complete right side of windscreen and canopy have been painted with the highly reflective white paint as I am to be positioned to the left of bomb blast and will be picking up maximum heat on the right side of aircraft. Skin under ailerons, flaps, and stabilizer also painted with varying shades of white. My visibility to my right is totally obscured. It has been a very hazardous flight condition that I have been forced to live with for the past seven flights but is necessary if I am to do everything possible to get the data the scientists are looking for. A 2-1/2 hour meeting was held with Capt. Deagan on Radist and the positioning of the F-84's, B-57, and F-101 in relation to the drop aircraft's being ahead or behind at 2 minutes to drop time. The B-52 pilot is supposed to call at 2 minutes to schedule drop time reporting whether he will be ahead or behind in time to drop. That means sudden critical changes that will have to be made by Radist control and my ability to adjust speed to gain or lose time. So far, it does not make me feel very comfortable. I sat in on a

Wright-Patterson test "Effects" aircraft fly-by for V.I.P.'s in Eniwetok before Cherokee bomb drop.

poker game for short time. Had two drinks with Joe Bourgorno (Republic Rep).

Thurs: D-1 May 10: *Briefing was held at 0930. Col. Samuels advised those of us who had flown through the first shot that this airburst of the large (5 megaton) bomb will be a different type of experience. As usual my position will be the closest to the bomb and the only "thermal aircraft" to be positioned tangential to the thermal wave. After lunch, we had our briefing with Capt. Mitchell, the Radist Project Officer. Following that, Kitch and I went spear fishing. Muster was called at 1630 and was called without prior notice so we were lucky that we returned to the barracks in time for the briefing. Maj. Anderson came through* for a check on us. People are becoming noticeably touchy and stay spring loaded in the "aggravated" position. We had Country Fried Steak for dinner. John, Kitch, and I had a drink at the club patio and when some of our engineers came by we got into a discussion of critical positioning. The admirals C-54 blew 3 tires at Bikini this evening and there is some concern as to whether they can get the aircraft repaired and off the island in time for the shot in the morning. The "Mook" handed me a spade that had washed up on the Coral Reef and said it was for me to start digging a hole to hide in, after he found out where I was to be positioned in the morning. Skipped the movie "No Angels We" as I have seen it and want to get some sleep. Most of bomber troops are in bed (2000) and at 2130 word received that we are officially at D-3. Bomber troops who had been bitching about the light being on when they thought they had to get up early, now were yakking and playing the radio and ignoring Kitch and my requests as we still had to get up at 0330 to fly more Radist practice flights.

Fri: D-3 May 11: Got up at 0300. Had steak and eggs (not much of a steak) took off at 0510. Flew voice controlled Radist and was within 0.8 seconds. Aircraft has only 1 hour and 35 minutes left on it until inspection so I logged only 45 minutes even though I flew 1 hour and 45 minutes. When we both arrived back over the island about the same time, Kitch and I swapped off wing positions doing some formation acrobatics to break the monotony of these long overwater flights. (We did not drop our wing tanks on the practice runs so we always had more fuel left on these flights than we had on the live missions where we dropped them. I had to fly on his right wing as my canopy is still completely painted over on the right side. Got back in bed at 0800 but shortly after that John took off with those two Pratt-

Whitney J-57 engines with afterburners going and rattled me out of bed.

I had a request to check radar site tracking. When I finished and as I was climbing out, Nan tower (north side of Eniwetok Atoll) called and said the detachment commander requested another pass if I had the fuel. I gave them a good one. Ran instrumentation calibration check for the Cook Laboratory troops and my full rudder kick with a drop tank on at 400 knots convinced me that I didn't want to try that maneuver again. Went to bed for a nap after lunch but was awakened by Captain Mitchell for a Radist meeting that lasted until 1830. Had free steak at the club as a result of winning the volleyball game. Had a long talk with Mr. Gibbs (the Radiation Corp. Project Manager) on the results of our Radist check flight and my lack of confidence in the system. (After all, my life depends on the accuracy of the system). Tried to get some sleep but partygoers woke me and we talked until 0030.

Wed: D-1 May 16: My flight cancelled because of a new shot scheduled for the next day. Radist wants time to try to correct problem with my system but won't have time to check it out in the air if shot actually goes tomorrow morning. Had another briefing for "Cherokee" and Col. Ousley made this announcement: "I don't want to know who did it but I was standing on the ramp yesterday with several Pentagon generals and some congressmen when one of our aircraft came in to land. The pilot performed an underneath three-quarter roll over the runway on the pitch-out and I was asked to explain such dangerous flying." He knew full well who it was and so did everyone else in the briefing room as I had been performing the three quarter right hand roll when making my left hand "break" for my 180 degree turn to the downwind leg of the traffic pattern ever since the right hand side of my windshield and canopy had been painted over. The first time I tried it, my ground crew got such a kick out of it that I continued to tell everyone that it was the only way I could visually clear my area before turning to the downwind leg of the traffic pattern. Of course, that wasn't the case as a roll to the right, as I was doing, had me rolling into the blind side of my vision but no one commented on that. Col. Ousley said for whoever it was not to do it again as long as there were V.I.P. on the island. Everything looks good for the shot tomorrow and after another lousy lunch, I helped "Robbie" tear down our 25 H.P. Evenrude outboard motor and scrape off the corrosion. It will be zinc chromated tomorrow. Went down to the office to look over my next "big bang" positioning. I found that the Cook Lab people had not been told about the new schedule for "Cherokee" going in the morning. They hadn't worked on the aircraft but that was "no sweat" as they had very little left to do. Kitch's airplane has mechanical problems and is out of commission and the ground crew is concerned that it won't be ready for tomorrow's shot. Part of the "H" bomb components were placed in one of our F-84 tent shelters. We had stopped using it because it was about to fall down. As soon as I heard they were being stored there I contacted Capt. Mitchell and he had them moved. I watched as they removed the bomb from the "broken" B-52 to the back-up drop aircraft (another B-52). I had to wonder how a device that small could create so much power and devastation. At 1600, Col. Cobb called a special briefing for effects aircraft crews and engineers. Looks as though the mission is still on for the morning. He kept all flight crewmembers for a special meeting on a rumor he had been told about some Radist pilots saying they would refuse to fly using the Radist positioning system. His lecture was on talking to the wrong people as the general approached him as to which pilots would have to be replaced. That was ridiculous as they couldn't replace anyone at this late date but I am happy that I have made it clear to everyone that although I lack confidence in the system, I will continue to help prove its reliability. No names were given out but I think the message got through to be careful whom you talk to about the project. One thing I am certain of is that the three fighter pilots are not the guilty parties. As I am the most critical aircraft relative to proximity to the bomb blast on all of the shots, I worry that someone may have used my name, but I am sure that all people close to the project know it wasn't me. Kitch flew a functional test flight (FTF) late in the afternoon and John and I went to dinner without him. We heard him land shortly after take-off and knew his bird still had problems. We expected to see him coming into the mess hall but when he hadn't arrived by show time John and I went to see the movie "The Jester." Just as the show started, we heard the F-84 start, taxi, and take-off and I knew Kitch was flying his FTF (Functional Test Flight) at night. He really wants to make the shot tomorrow. We all knew each one we missed would mean staying longer to participate in the last shots. After the movie, we stopped by the club and played a few hands of Black Jack. John won $5.00 and I managed to come out $3.00 ahead. "A first!" Found it hard to get any sleep thinking about getting back into action after all of the practice and aborted missions. Reminds me of the night before a flack suppression mission on a very hot target such as Pyongyang or the bridge at Sinuiju.

Thurs: D-0 May 18: *Bomber troops were up at 0100 and I got up at 0300 but didn't get much sleep during the night. Had my steak* *and eggs and then filed my clearance at Test Operations before heading to our project office. Just before leaving Operations, I was told we had gone back to D-1 because of B-52 drop aircraft problems. Another source said that it was because of winds at 12,000 feet being unfavorable for fall-out. Any way my mind has become numb and that knot of frustration in my stomach is getting tighter from all of the start and stop that has been associated with airdrop mission. It is the only subject of discussion anywhere on the island and I'm tired of hearing it. Col. Ousley said in his meeting yesterday that none of us is acting completely normal anymore and it is only natural after living under the strain we have had for the last several months. There are just not enough outlets for the tension we are living under day after day. I should feel pretty lucky just to be able to get off the island while flying but those overwater flights add a different level of tension. I had just gotten back in bed when the bombers that were already in the air before the cancellation, began landing. Shortly thereafter, Tom Sumner, the B-47 pilot came in and asked if I would take his duty officer post. It was really mine but he owed me one and was going to take it for me. I couldn't refuse so I dressed and went to the office. Not much activity except I was able to get our telephone repaired. Col. Cobb dropped by and seeing me on duty said that flight crew didn't have to stand duty on shot days. Spent the afternoon painting a picture for Tracy's room (my oldest daughter). Lost our volleyball game. Heard Joe Huddle, Robbies B-66 crew chief was being operated on for intestinal ulcer. He was on operating table for 4-1/2 hours but the outlook is good. It's no surprise that he had ulcers and I think there are a lot of candidates among us for the same. After supper and a drink, John, Kitch, Joe, Santi (another Republic rep) and I went to see the "Far Country."*

Fri: D-0 May 19: *Same routine as night before except for rain, which was pouring down in buckets. My artificial horizon would not level itself and I had to abort and was relieved to hear mission had been cancelled. John came into the office and asked what the "Mook's" call sign was. One of the B-57's crew had bailed out and search and rescue aircraft were looking for the crew. They found the pilot but not the radar observer. They were part of the sampler aircraft group that flew around the cloud to measure radiation levels as it drifted towards the east. They live in the room next to mine. He was supposed to go back to the states today. They thought they had spotted his one-man life raft but when rescue reached the spot, it turned out to be just a floating box. Worked on Tracy's picture. Talked to Capt. Hall, pilot of the B-57 that had engine failure, which sounded similar to the one I had and has been plaguing all aircraft using the J-65 engines. I am certainly not convinced that I am free of another possible engine failure when flying through super-cooled moisture, which causes the shroud ring around the turbine wheel to shrink and rub turbine blades, causing the failure. It sounds like Halls aircraft suffered the same failure as mine. Flying under the hood, I could not see the clouds that I might fly through and therefore I am unable to comply with the flight safety directive that prohibits flying unmodified engine F-84's through visible moisture that is below zero degrees centigrade. Rain was too heavy to sit through a movie so came home and got a couple of hours sleep. John and Kitch woke me up and I went to the club for a nightcap. Checked mail for everyone in our barracks. Had two letters from Evie and a box of candy from my folks. Wrote two letters and then back to bed.*

Sun: D-1 May 20: *Another miserable rainy day. Got up about*

1100 and went to lunch with Santi Arenas and Joe B. (Republic Reps). I was scheduled to fly this afternoon so I couldn't go over to "Glen Island" with all of the rest of the troops. About an hour after they left the weather cancelled me out from flying. Spent all afternoon writing and reading. After supper, I had a meeting with Stan Novak (Wright Field Engineer), John, Kitch, Santi, Joe, and two other project men. It ended up in a heated discussion on the J-65 engine flying in moisture and I am convinced that these engines we are flying are not safe in the kind of heavy moisture we are encountering while flying at some of the altitudes our flight profiles require. It is an exercise in futility as I am going to have to fly them regardless of the extra risk I know we are taking. Most of my missions are at night and under my light proof hood therefore I can't tell if I am in clouds or not! Went to a movie and then to bed.

Mon: D-0 May 21: Got a good night's sleep until 0310. (Didn't even hear bomber troops get up). Had my steak and eggs and then my regular routine of operations, project office and then to the flight line. I've gotten this routine down pat as I have had enough practice in the past two weeks. Everything was running on schedule but past record has me unsure that they will drop today. My night take-off with one-drop tank into that inky blackness over the water was pretty hairy, particularly as I was not sure of the accuracy of my new fight attitude indicator. I cut the base line at point "Fred" and proceeded on my northeasterly heading. My first attempt to contact Radist was successful and they said they were picking me up "just fine!" When I asked for an Azimuth and progress check, nothing moved on either of my needles. Following several more unsuccessful attempts to send me guidance information, they asked if I would accept voice control into the target. I had never tried flying Azimuth and was *not sure that they could give me progress and Azimuth guidance to time "zero" and stay within safe limits but I said that if that's all we had I'd give it a try. About six minutes to go until bomb blast, I stopped receiving guidance information. I waited about one and a half minutes and then asked if they were still on the air.*

Shortly thereafter, the Radist controller told all Radist aircraft to abort the mission as they had lost all guidance information. This most certainly saved my life but I was mad as hell after agreeing to take the risk of following their voice commands and after all of the extra effort my crew and I had made to be ready for this mission, including my flying with the one side of vision blind for so many flights, and then having to abort. I listened with great interest as I flew away from Bikini on a vector to the west-southwest towards Eniwetok. I was hoping something would prevent the drop and they would abort this try but as I listened on the radio, I heard the bombardier calling his time to drop countdown. I couldn't believe it, when following my countdown clock, he went from 1 minute 30 seconds to drop, and within 10 seconds, he called 45 seconds to drop. These calls came in loud and clear to my headset but the B-47, B-52B, and B-66 crews said they were too garbled to tell what was said. Then came the code words from the drop B-52, "complete" this meant that the bomb was released and falling towards its target. The real problem was that it was released about 45 seconds too early! Robinette in the B-66 wisely aborted at the first garbled call and although he was heading in the opposite direction from the drop aircraft, would have been in some danger from the fireball and would have received the shock wave at a much higher force and from a different direction than expected. He very likely would not have had a "complete" aircraft under his control thereafter.

All of the other aircraft that aborted were heading in the same direction as the B-66 but all of those machines as was the B-66, were offset to one side and were not flying directly towards the place where the bomb actually exploded.

I had pulled my hood back and knew I was well out of range of any blast or heat effects from the bomb but I was really surprised by the intensity of the flash. I was in the clouds and at least 10 miles from it. It seemed as though my mind had stopped functioning and had missed part of the countdown when, after about 1 minute the bombardiers voice came on the radio and obviously he thought he was on intercom, talking to the pilot. Instead, he was broadcasting to the world as the V.I.P. observer's ships loud speakers were all tuned into the count-down. The bombardier sounded confused and started apologizing for dropping too soon and he rambled on for several minutes while those listening began to boil inside. Kitch was the only Radist aircraft to successfully complete the mission but he was too far from the blast for the data to be of much value. After landing, I attended an emergency debriefing. First of all, the Radist system that was needed to control me had gone down because a worker on an island where one of my transmitting towers was located, backed a tractor into the antenna tower knocking it down. Secondly, the bomb was dropped 5 miles short of the target area and 45 seconds early. That meant that at 45 seconds before I was to be five miles left of the bomb explosion, it would have gone off directly in front of me. I would have flown into the fireball and never have known I was doing so until I was fried like a French fried potato. The other aircraft were to be in positions to the south of the blast and as the drop ship was flying on basically a north to south course when it dropped 5 miles short meant the other test aircraft were too far south of the blast to get any meaningful data.

I know that the drop crew landed and refueled across the runway from our area and left as soon as they could. I heard that they had given the crew distinguished flying crosses, which greatly degraded the ones given for true outstanding flying accomplishment. It must have already been written up and were probably awarded for publicity purposes, I can tell you it did nothing for the morale of those of us who were doing our jobs the way we were supposed to. We had a big meeting this afternoon on the B-52 screw-up and the positioning of each of our aircraft on the next shot "Zuni." Capt. Mitchell wants to tear into my instrumentation bridges and repair some of the strain gauges. I told them to do it before "Cherokee" as there was not as much chance that we would get good data on the drop mission. He didn't listen and it looks as though I might miss "Zuni" where chances of getting good data would be very good.

This log should give a small idea as to the frustration that we had to deal with during the entire stay on "The Rock" as it was referred to by all of us after being isolated on it for a while. It was like being in prison without ever committing a crime. In fact, today the criminal has T.V., telephones, and weekend visits with their families or girlfriends. We tried our best to solve the boredom problem and had brought a lot of recreational things with us on the bombers where they had room to carry them. We were actually much better prepared than a lot of the other 3,000 men calling Eniwetok home. Those of us participating in the "Effects" flight testing had an additional stress factor and Kitch and I had another concern by having only one engine *carrying us over all of those miles of ocean. That brings me to my two other stress factors the others didn't have and they were: my route carrying me over 260 miles from the closest surface ship or rescue aircraft on my flights to Bikini and then getting there I had the most critical positioning by always being closer to the bomb blast than any other participating aircraft, ship, or person. I always considered myself as a fairly stable and adjustable person.*

A copy of the poster "Our Lone Woman on Eniwetok" (so we don't forget).

In my combat tours in Korea, I flew my two tours in the first truly operational jet fighter in the United States and helped establish the rules and procedures for jet fighter combat tactics, having started flying in the Korean conflict the day after the North invaded South Korea. The majority of my missions were in ground support where you are exposed to enemy ground fire, inhospitable terrain and all types of bad weather. Our food was lousy and even the ground troops passing through K-2 from the front lines chose to heat their C-rations on the engines of their jeeps rather than eat our mess hall prepared food. We all slept in our tents inside sleeping bags zipped almost completely closed with our 45 caliber automatics laying just inside the small opening in the unzipped part. North Korean guerrillas would sneak past our South Korean guards (who generally stood guard duty close to the warm fire barrels) and slipped into a few tents at night and randomly slit the throats of those sleeping in the tent. The next morning the demoralizing effect on the people who tried to wake their buddy and found him with his throat cut was devastating. I found that I handled these conditions and flew more combat missions in a shorter period of time than any other pilot in my squadron. When Fifth Air Force placed a limit on the combat missions for fighters at 100, I was already past 110. Our group commander stated that no one could extend their tour without the approval of the squadron commander and final approval had to be his. I felt fortunate to be one of the few pilots who was allowed to stay for a second tour. I could see the help we were giving to the men doing the tough fighting on the ground and I felt totally in charge of my tactics. I led most of the missions I flew. I point this out to show how much more stressful this tour of duty on Eniwetok was for me. I knew what needed to be done to expedite the process of getting the needed data but things such as fixing the instrumentation before "Cherokee" after all of the attempts and special efforts on my part (such as being willing to fly the live mission on voice control from Radist when we had never tried it before). So many things that unknowingly sneak up on you and create internal trauma from the continuous pressures, get a reaction of some kind from the old body, and mine came first as severe stomach pains. The doctor gave me some G.I. medicine and told me not to drink any alcohol.

* * * * *

From the day after "Cherokee" I received the disturbing news that the instrumentation on my bird would have to be partially removed, which was major surgery for the maintenance and instrumentation crews. It certainly meant that I was going to miss "Zuni" unless it was cancelled at least two or three times. That night after I had gotten to sleep, the bomber troops, who had steaks on the radiation company, came in well oiled, and woke John and me up to go water-skiing with them. We told them they were nuts and after hearing them head for the recreation beach where our boat was docked we got up and followed them down. By the time we arrived, the boat was disappearing into the blackness of the lagoon. They had sense enough to put on life vests but I was concerned that if they fell off, George, who was driving the boat, couldn't find them and might run over them in the dark. The other factor was the coral trees that in some cases were just inches under the surface of the water and could be distinguished by a dark shadow in the daytime could not be seen at night. If you ran over one at night, it would tear the bottom out of the boat and tear up a skier's body. As they say, "The good Lord looks after fools and drunks," and there were a lot of both that night. Luckily, none of the bad things happened and we were able to work off some steam until the M.P.'s showed up. John and I were back in our pick-up truck when we saw them coming and drove to the barracks. Shortly thereafter, the jeep arrived with the rest of our troops being escorted by two M.P. jeeps. They tried to accuse us of stealing government property for unauthorized use. They didn't know what to do when they found out that we owned the boat. I expected some repercussion from it but nothing was ever said and we did not try that escapade again.

Wed: D-5 May 23: Went down to the flight line this morning and talked with Col. Cobb about tearing into my airplane to work on instrumentation. He is in favor of doing it. We also talked about Radist reliability and he told me there was a meeting over at "Perry Island" (where laboratory and Task Force headquarters is located) and they are discussing the problem. (Interesting that none of the flight crews who are flying the system are invited.) He told me that they are going to bring their equipment over here to calibrate our sets. They are also talking about getting a new chief over here, but I don't think that is their problem. It appears as though the instrumentation system in my bird is pretty well messed up and doesn't look as though I will make the big "Z" shot if it goes on time. Talked to Mitchell about working crews 24 hours in shifts but he was already working on it.

Thu: D-4 May 24: Arose this morning to be greeted by the most disheartening news since we arrived (and that's saying a lot!) They are going to have to tear into my aircraft on the left side, take out the instrumentation, and replace all of it. It took months to install it at the factory in Chicago, so doing it in the field is going to be really difficult. I feel for the "Cook" troops who are working on it under the conditions they have to deal with here.

This could take a long time and will probably cause me to miss one or two shots. The weather officer says the weather will be bad for the "Z" shot every day for the rest of the month as the upper winds are too strong. He stated that he did not see that it would be possible to get all of the shots off by the scheduled cut-off date. John's F-101 is "AOCP" (out of commission for lack of available parts) so he requested that he and I be allowed to take a few days leave in Hawaii. Col. Cobb said he would check for us. Afternoon was spent swimming and early evening in volleyball tournament. No mail for second scheduled mail plane in a row. Saw "Ulysses" at the movie for second time and still enjoyed it. Received some academic books addressed to me and assume they are Bob Mercers to keep for him until he arrives. After the movie, John, Kitch, and I went to the club and met some of the radiation people. Mr. Gibbs showed me where I would have been if they had not gone off the air on the "Cherokee" shot. I would have been right in the corner of the fireball. Someone "up there" must be looking out for me. I hope that whatever I am being kept here on Earth for is going to be for a good cause.

Fri: D-3 May 25: Checked on aircraft and instrumentation progress and am pleased that work is coming along faster than expected. They are still fighting to get ready for "Z" but shot will have to be delayed at least two days for me to have any chance of being ready. Nothing from Col. Cobb on our leave request. John and I launched the boat and went spear fishing and shell hunting in some pretty deep water just before the dark blue drop off. The water really does turn cold when you reach the edge of that center of the volcano. Saw a poor show tonight "Strangers Hand." (I am now becoming a movie critic.)

Sat: D-2 May 26: Another dragged out day with very little to do *that is productive. Painted a little and wrote progress?? Letter to the Fighter Section but had to tear it up as we have been ordered not to discuss the B-52 drop ships "goof." Had a "Z" briefing this afternoon, John, and I got a fairly large "killer clam" and with the help of several other people were able to drag it ashore. It must weigh 500 to 600 pounds once it is out of the water and the muscles that hold the "jaws" together are almost impossible to cut. Went to a double feature, "Court Martial of Billy Mitchell" and "Passion." When I got back to the room there was a letter from Maj. Wade from the Fighters at W-P and it doesn't look as though there is any move to replace us as had been discussed prior to our leaving to come out here.*

Sun: D-1 May 27: *Kitch flew early. John and I went to Glen Island— the one across the inlet— and it is just like the South Sea tropical paradise that you see in the travel brochures and movies. There is a beautiful jungle that is shaded by tall coconut palms laden with coconuts. The coral reef had many beautiful formations with killer clams, sharks, and moray eels. Kitch came over and put on a good show for us. We found quite a few pretty and unusual shells. When we got back, we went to the Beach Club for drinks and steaks on Republic. Also, found that we cannot eat the coconuts due to fear that they have been affected by the radiation from all of the bomb testing that has been conducted here on Eniwetok in the past several years. The same applies to anything we catch in the sea.*

Mon: D-0 May 28: *Got up this morning for an early breakfast. John and I saw all of the troops off to their respective aircraft and then went back to bed. We got up in time to see the shot. It was mighty impressive as it lit up the dark night sky as though it was daylight and that was from 230 miles away. Radist screwed* up again and had Kitch 30 miles short where he didn't get any useful data. Major Anderson (Bomber Andy) had conned Col. Cobb into approving his request to land at Hickham in Honolulu if the shot reached its predicted yield, as they were "afraid" that they might have damage that would make landing on our short airstrip here at Eniwetok too dangerous. Unfortunately, for them the yield was lower than predicted and they returned home. Hard to understand why the good Col. has ignored John's and my request for legitimate leave but I guess it comes from obtaining rank through technical knowledge rather than through command assignments. They have torn into the other wing of my F-84 and removed another fuel cell. (A fairly major maintenance procedure.) No telling when I will be back in the air. The maintenance and instrumentation people are working as hard as they can. They don't want to spend any more time on this island than I do. Went shell hunting over at Sand Island with John but my coral wounds I suffered at Glen Island yesterday hurt too much when I got into the salt water so I bagged the spear fishing and just walked the reef. The baby moray eels, which were almost transparent except for the eyes and teeth, showed me what you face if one of the eels ever grabs hold of you. I would get one of those 6-inch babies to bite the end of my metal spear and once they latched onto it the only way they would let go was when the lower jaw tore away from the rest of the head. Won our volleyball game (on a forfeit), went to the club, and lost a fast $1.00 playing Ship-Captain-and-Crew. Saw the "Golden Mistress" and came back to the room. Mail arrived but not much for me. Watched the B-52 and B-47 crews pack for leave in Honolulu. No explanation from Col. Cobb. I guess he thinks that the poor fellows are overworked and deserve leave more than John and I do.

Tues: May 29: *Spent most of the morning down on the flight line checking on progress with my F-84. It is doubtful if it will be ready for the next shot: "Flat." Instrumentation is progressing slowly on their work. Took PM duty officer for John. Bomber troops all left for Hawaii. Talked with Major Harmon, the base flying safety officer about our flying with the unmodified J-65 engines and found that he knew nothing about my engine failure and dead stick landing. Amazing! Had supper and went to the club. Most of maintenance troops were there with Ralph Stevens who was out of the hospital. He said he felt bad about leaving for home but I don't think too many people really believe that. Mail was fouled up and ours was left at Kwagalin by mistake. John Boughman and Rudy came by and woke me up and when John and Kitch showed up, we had a noisy party until some ungodly hour.*

Wed: May 30: *Memorial Day. Got up early and after breakfast went down to the flight line to see John and Kitch off on their flights. John's part came in and he is back among the clouds. The shot was a small nuclear device exploded in the air out over the lagoon. It was interesting but not very impressive compared to those large hydrogen bombs we have previously been exposed to. Went back to bed for an hour and then got up and went on a picnic to Japtan Island, the Navy's recreation island. Typical military recreation area with signs all over the place saying "off limits" or "don't" do this or that. Our group had a pretty nice time but not much new except good steaks and lots of beer. The Navy troops from one of the ships that had just anchored in the lagoon showed up and started their party. It wasn't long before they were passed out all over the area and being carried or helped back to their launches. We came back by way of a couple of ships dropping off some of the Navy men who were ready to leave their* parties. Went to the club for a couple of drinks. The trip was fun and helped a little to break the monotony but I still feel the built up tension and depression of helplessness. I can't do my job until the other people do theirs right and so far I know I have done everything possible to accomplish mine and have accomplished almost nothing productive. Even the leave in Hawaii would have been frustrating as I would still be in a state of limbo. I need to get back in the air and on to whatever the conclusion of these tests have waiting for me!

Thu: Day 31: Gloomy day. Time passes slowly no matter how hard we try to find activities to keep us busy. Not much sleep last night but I have my sleep schedule so mixed up that it is no real surprise. Aircraft is still out of commission.

Fri: June 1: Still no flying with aircraft out. Start of another month and things are looking better for schedule staying as is.

Sat: June 2: Lt. Bob Mercer arrived today—brought news from home. Went to the club and "had a few." Still no sleep for some reason. Nerves seem to be all tense from being on the ground so long with nothing productive to do.

Sun: June 3: Wrote several letters and tried to sleep while everyone was on the boat. Not much success in sleep attempt. Stomach doesn't feel hungry and I feel all tied up in a knot.

Mon: June 4: Tracy's 3rd birthday. Spent the morning checking the progress on the F-84 and then went swimming all afternoon. Saw "The Bridges at Tokori" (pretty good). Slept pretty good but woke up at 0600.

Tue: June 5: Evie and my 8th anniversary. Spent most of the day down at the flight line trying to help put the bird back together. The troops have really worked very hard on accomplishing a task that should have been done in the aircraft factory or major aircraft depot. I am going to see that they all get a good letter of appreciation put in the personnel files. Got back into the air at 1645 and had permission to put on a show at Japtan Island. Just about all of the Wright-Patterson (WADC) troops except for my maintenance crew, were there for a picnic. Made a couple of good passes with rolls followed by loop and Cuban eight. Our guys were on the boat heading home and missed it. I inadvertently "boomed" the base and everyone thought it was the F-101, but John was on the boat and that really confused them. Most of the people weren't aware that the F-84 could go super-sonic. The flight did wonders for me and my tensions are greatly relieved. Saw a poor movie "A Creature Walks Among Us."

Wed: June 6: Flew 3 flights. One Radist practice without telemetering. Had voice control only and came out pretty close to on time and I was pleased with the results. Kitch and I flew a formation acrobatic flight and then we flew a WADC aircraft formation which included all of our effects test aircraft. (B-52, B-57, B-47, B-66, F-101A, and the two F-84F's. The Navy A-3D was also with us). After the fly-by, Kitch and I put on a show performing formation acrobatics over the field. We looked good according to all the compliments we received after landing. It certainly felt good to me and I can't tell you how good it feels to be flying again even in these tough conditions. Saw "Conquest of Space" and visited the club. A few of us returned to barracks and our noisy party disturbed some of the "T.A.C. bomber crews" in the next room. None of us were too heartbroken over it.

Thu: June 7: *Flew two Radist flights to Bikini. (+.3 sec. and -.1 sec). The first had voice control only and the second flight the guidance system worked good all the way for the first time since we arrived in March! Bob Mercer and I had a couple of drinks at the club after supper and then went to see "Square Jungle." John Boughman dropped by the room later in the evening well on his way to "happy land." He and the rest of the ground crew have been working awfully hard and I think "The Rock" is getting to them. With just reason, I might add.*

Fri: D-2 June 8: *Flew good Radist mission and I believe they are nailing down the system. Finally, Kitch flew my aircraft this afternoon and agrees with me that it is very unstable and it has a very disturbing yaw just before the stall. On landing, the left wing dropped sharply and he hit on the left wheel hard enough to blow the tire on that wheel. On the way home from the club tonight John, Bob, Rudy, and I found a large chunk of ice and had probably the only snowball fight ever held on Eniwetok! We had walked out on the movie "Devils Harbor" because it was so bad: No mail today.*

Sat: D-1 June 9: *No flying today. We were briefed in the morning for tomorrow's shot. Went to the B.X., looked at sport coats after lunch, and spent the rest of the afternoon swimming. Muster called at 1615 and we were advised that we were now D-2. Movie was too crowded so came back to room and wrote letter home. I went to the second feature "Kiss of Fire," not much to it.*

Sun: D-2 June 10: *Went down to fly in P.M. but Radist was off the air. In the afternoon, we all went out to Sand Island. We towed another boat with us so that everyone could go. John shot* a 20-pound grouper after Mercer had ruined two spears on it. Movie was "The Indian Fighter."

Mon: D-1 June 11: Day started out as D-1 for shot at Eniwetok and D-2 for Bikini shot. Flew one Bikini mission with good Radist results (-.1 sec). I was duty officer in the afternoon and while on duty we went D-1 on the Bikini shot (Flathead). Went to see "The Benny Goodman Story." I started writing a letter but went to sleep before I finished it.

Tues: D-0 June 12: Got up at 0330 and just after I had finished shaving, the bomber troops came in saying "F" had been cancelled. I wasn't going to get any sleep so we went to breakfast. John was flying in Blackfoot so I knew Kitch and I weren't going to get any sleep anyway. During breakfast, they announced that Flathead was back "on" and confusion became rampant, particularly with the bomber crews. A.O.C. didn't know what the "H" hour would be for quite some time after the new announcement. The B-57 reported hitting something on the runway on take-off. They had to send jeeps out on the strip to check and that threw more confusion and delays into the works. I was 4 minutes late on my take-off and I was really burning about the possibility that I might miss another shot because of someone else's screw-up. I had to work at convincing myself that it would be possible to make up that much time by pushing the power up to 100% and cutting the first leg of the course by 10 degrees. When I made the intercept of the final leg, I was just about on time. I ran into some heavy turbulence on the final run at 6 minutes-to-go that added to the difficulty in holding heading and progress. I was 0.35 seconds early but the yield was a little higher than predicted and I should have good data. Kitch checked me over when I arrived back over the base and couldn't see any real damage.

After I landed, we found that the thinner metal under the wing flaps, ailerons, and stabilator had been so hot that they were brittle to the point that you could punch holes through them with your finger. The black electrician tape that was wrapped around the wiring and mount on my over-the-shoulder camera was scorched. That camera was inside the cockpit just above my right shoulder but I didn't remember feeling any excessive heat although it had to have gotten pretty hot while I was covering my eyes and verifying that I could see all of the bones in my hand. My tailbone really hurt from the impact of the shock wave. The calibrated "g" meter doesn't mean much to me as each shot it has "pegged-out" at + 22 "g's"and minus 6 g's. Went to the B.X. and bought some task force "7" souvenir Zippo lighters for gifts. Slept for a few hours in the afternoon and then went to supper. Met "Zeigler" (a former Air Force fighter pilot who was stationed with me at Rome AFB, New York in the 1st Fighter group and now works for E.G.G. Corporation) and had a nice visit with him. Saw "Quenton Durward" at the show and then came back to write some letters.

Wed: June 13: *Uneventful day. Slept late and then went swimming in the afternoon. Went to see "Track of the Cat" after eating supper and then went back to the club but only drank 7-Up as my stomach is really hurting. The chow is getting worse and on top of that (or because of it) one of the cooks used his meat cleaver on one of the K.P.'s head and left him in pretty serious condition. My F-84 is out of commission while the engineers make some static loads test on the strain gauges to calibrate them for accuracy.*

Thu: June 14: *Rained most of the day. John flew in MA-1 Air-to-Air missile warhead explosion over the lagoon. I watched through* my dark glasses and it was a "pretty little booger." Bought some sterling silver knives and perfume at the B.X. I took Robbie's duty officer in P.M., which gave me an opportunity to write my dad for Father's Day. Weather has become extremely "muggy."

Fri: June 15: Today was a big day as John and I flew on the photo C-54 to Kwajalein. It was my first time off "The Rock" since I arrived in March and the first time I had seen a woman in as long. We stopped long enough to run to the B.X. and snack bar for a hamburger and to see and hear live female women. Amazing what just seeing and talking to them does for my morale. John was with me and his comments were the same as mine. After the short stay at "Kwag," we continued down to the tiny island of Majuro. It is the territorial governmental headquarters for the Marshall Islands and as we approached it, I was astounded at the tropical beauty I saw from my vantage point in the co-pilot seat. The pilot let me land the big machine on the coral runway that was carved out of the palm trees on an angle at the fattest part on the southeastern end of the half-moon shaped atoll. We were met by Mr. White and Mr. Leonard ? from the U.S. Department of Interior. Leonard ? took us to his quarters for a drink. While riding in the jeep through this sleepy little village, everyone I saw was either sleeping or resting on the steps or porches of their huts or against the trunk of a palm tree.

No one paid too much attention to our passing except for an occasional finger to the brim of a pulled down straw hat as a greeting to Leonard. This was almost exactly what the movie people had always depicted in their tropical paradise scenes. There were a couple of two-masted interisland sailing ships anchored out in the lagoon. There was one old diesel powered motor ship tied to the one small pier but no activity of any kind except our parade of two jeeps slowly bouncing over the coral bumps on the unpaved paths through the village. The scent of the tropical flowers hung tantalizingly in the breathless warm South Pacific air and gave off an air of total peace and isolation from the cares of the outside world.

Across the lagoon was the remnant of a sunken Japanese cargo ship but nothing else that would indicate there had ever been a war in this part of the Pacific. When I asked Leonard about the island's history during the war, he told me that the Japanese had a military stronghold on the island to the east several miles away but for some reason had never paid much attention to Majuro. The whole atmosphere was one that made you know that time passed for these people without having too much meaning. Each day almost the same as the one before with plenty to eat and drink until the United States decided to make this tiny outpost the headquarters for the government of the Marshall Islands.

The commissioner's wife and 21-year-old daughter were away in Honolulu on vacation but I met Mrs. Fischer, wife of the hotel and messing facilities director. It was great to be able to sit down and have an intelligent conversation with a woman after these months of seeing only one WAF (Women's Air Force) Sergeant who passed through Eniwetok on a General's aircraft and had to get coffee and sandwiches from the Mess Hall. (She arrived and left under armed guard.) The stop in "Kwag" only gave me the few moments to order a sandwich and ask a few questions about the island. Sitting down to a luncheon on a table set with silverware, tablecloth and crystal glassware was not what I expected but I guess it gave the wives who had to adjust to this lifestyle a chance to keep in touch with their heritage by bringing civilization to their cottages whenever outside westerners stopped by.

The supply C-54 came in once a month and it, according to Mrs. Fischer, was a chance to entertain in a small way. To us it was like we were honored guests at a banquet. All too soon, we had to say good-bye to our wonderful host and hostess and work our way back towards the airport. I tried to absorb as much into my conscious observation cells to capture in my mind what I could of the real charm of this hidden paradise. I'm sure I wouldn't want a full diet of it but the quaint little Quonset cottages and butler type houses snuggled back among the thick forest of palm trees were unique. They had electricity and the refrigerators stood outside on the ground or on the porch when there was one. There were a few old-fashioned washing machines with wringers attached to the side but aside from those extravagances, I felt there was little that these people needed from the outside world. I didn't find out what the native population was but there were a few Hawaiians, Filipinos and mainlanders. Their schedules were pretty loose as they mostly traveled by interisland boats. I bought some unusually beautiful "cowry" shells at the trading post and while I was there, I asked if the natives did much spear fishing for food. The native manager of the store told me that they very seldom went in the water and when I commented on the plentiful shark population as a deterrent, he told me that they were not afraid of the sharks but were afraid of moray eels.

We took off and as we circled the island and headed back to "Kwag" I noticed several outrigger canoes in the lagoon and another village all the way at the opposite end of the island. I felt that I would have loved to spend 3 or 4 days exploring the atoll but we were on our way back to the realities of why we were out in this part of the world. I wondered whether I would ever get back to spend time on the island that had so captured my fancy. After a stop back on Kawgalien and a great supper, we trudged slowly in the old "Sky master" to our home away from home to settle down to start working again in the morning. It was a break from our boredom and did wonders for my morale as it did for John's.

Sat: June 16: Flew Radist tape and was -0.5 seconds and will have to be re-flown. Day changed from D-3 to D-2. John flew to Tarawa on a supply aircraft and didn't know about the change. Movie was a good one, "Patterns."

Sun: D-1 June 17: After our briefing, I spent all morning trying to get into the air. The runway was closed all morning because of crash equipment removing the C-124 mail plane that crashed on landing last night. (As I mentioned earlier in chapter.) In the afternoon, the fuel trucks were low on fuel. I finally started my taxi out at 1430 when a "Cambridge" C-97 landed long, blew all of its main wheel tires, and closed the runway until 1800. Had good Radist flight but ran out of oxygen and had an interesting flight home at low altitude. Saw a B-36 heading home to the land of the big B.X. and wished him a good trip in fighter fashion. I think he'll remember the details of the F-84F plan form as it flashed straight up in front of his nose while rolling skyward. Gene Dietrick had gotten some steaks and I had helped start the fire before I left to fly. When I got back, there were two waiting for me. I got to bed early and had a good night's sleep until 0330.

Mon: D-0 June 18: Had my steak and eggs and went to the flight line to tell ground crew to put on the 2-drop tanks (external fuel tanks under the wing which can be jettisoned). After briefing, I climbed up into the cockpit, but installing the drop tank was causing a problem and crew was running behind schedule. I finally signaled them to drop them and I would chance making it without them. Just about then, I received a call on the radio telling me we had slipped to D-2 and the shot was scrubbed. I scheduled a flight for "in-flight loads testing" of the strain gauges. Just before take-off at noon, I had to cancel as we went to D-1. Swam most of the afternoon after adjusting the schedule. Water was cool and relaxing. John, Kitch, and I had a few nips on an empty stomach and then after eating, John and I went to see "Kismet," then back to the room for some sleep.

Tues: D-0 June 19: The mission was moved to D-2 during the night and day was totally uneventful. Saw "Miracle in the Rain" and it was appropriate as it rained on us during part of the show.

Wed: D-2 June 20: Mission slipped one day again, with nothing better to do. I asked Col. Cobb how much delay en route we were authorized on our return trip and as I suspected he couldn't give an answer until checking with Fighter Ops at Wright-Patterson. John, Kitch, and I knew the answer and had no idea when (or if) we would be going back, but it pays to plan ahead. Even when you know you won't get an answer. I tried to see the flight surgeon about my stomach but he was operating.

Thurs: D-1 June 21: Stopped by the flight surgeon's on the way to my aircraft but he was out of the office. Flew practice Radist flight and then made inverted pass down the runway followed by a Cuban "8." The Ops. Officer restricted me to 400 feet above the strip but I think he would have had a hard time judging the exact height although he said he thought I was too low. The ground troops, John, and Kitch, said it looked great! Slept most of the afternoon and then went to have a drink and supper with Kitch and Max Christianson from Douglas. Max gave me a job application and the name of someone at Douglas Aircraft

Company in Santa Monica, California he wanted me to stop and talk to on my way home. Saw "Anything Goes" and came back to barracks. Three mail planes arrived today and everyone got letters except for me. I hope everything is all right at home.

Fri: D-1/2 June 22: Got up at 0330 and had steak and eggs. Take-off was at 0524 and everything went smoothly even when H-Hour was shifted back 20 minutes. I adjusted to an orbiting pattern 9 minutes out and then when I was on track for live run, the mission was scrubbed with 7 minutes to go. Came back and had heavy rain over the island and had to squeeze enough fuel out of the tanks to make it in for an instrument landing between the big aircraft that had plenty of fuel. Got home to bed and slept until mid-afternoon. Finally!

Sat: D-? June 23: Had duty officer chore all day. Filled out job application for Douglas Aircraft Company but don't really think I will turn it in. Now that is a sign of the ultimate boredom! After a poor supper, I played Blackjack at the club and lost $3.50 so the day continued as a washout. I had seen the movie so went back to the room.

Sun: D-? June 24: Got up for breakfast to feed my ulcer as it is the only meal that I know that the cooks can't mess up too much. I returned to the room and played a long game of chess with Ed Little, the B-66 navigator/bombardier. Bob Mercer stopped by and talked me into going spear fishing. A large group of us (10) went to a reef in the lagoon that had a beautiful white sandy bottom and clear water. We had to tow a special services' boat behind our powerboat so that all of us could go. It was a fun afternoon except for the few seconds when a shark startled me by swimming under me when my spear gun was unloaded. After we returned, I saw a copy of the "shot" timetable and am very discouraged at the outlook of only two shots during the next two months. I guess the idea of doing nothing productive for long periods of time with only one productive test flight a month is just not part of my working lifestyle. John and I started planning a way to have our wives meet us in Honolulu on our way home and staying for several weeks if we are close enough to getting our credit for an overseas tour.

Mon: D-? June 25: *Flew a practice Radist mission carrying two drop tanks and timing was good. On the way home I bounced what I thought was a lone F-84G (straight-wing) sampler. I was surprised to find that while I was on the first aircraft's tail the second one was closing in on mine. We started at 15,000 feet, which is a fairly low altitude for my machine, and they gave me a good fight. The only way I could shake both of them was to accelerate away from them. Not very sporting but you have to use the tools that work. When I was back in the Eniwetok area, I flew the dynamic loads tests on the strain gauge instrumentation and then landed uneventfully. Slept most of the afternoon. After supper, I worked on a "whistle" for my F-84 to install on one of my external tank fittings. It should make a great screaming noise as I make my high-speed passes over the runway.*

Tue: D-0 June 26: *Up at 0330. Didn't get a full night's sleep as the rats that we hear scrambling around on the roof and on the metal rafters in our room must have been amorous or fighting around midnight. Anyway, they woke me with all of the noise and then when one landed on my sheet I leaped out of my upper bunk and probably beat him to the floor. Several other people jumped out of bed as they had heard the rats' commotion and when I threw off my sheet, and probably the rat, and hit the* floor, they joined me. When I turned on the light, we could see the tails of two or three scurrying away on the upper rafters. The one that was momentarily trapped in my sheet, which was now on the floor, came out in a dazed pattern causing those of us standing on the floor to jump to higher ground. (Footnote: You would think that a small island such as this with 3,000 men on it would be able to eliminate the rat population but we never did and they are probably still populating the building that may still be there).

Ate my usual "last breakfast" and followed the "shot morning" routine. After starting the engine and waiting for my taxi time, I also waited to hear that the shot had been cancelled. Finally, I was cleared to taxi for take-off and then I was rolling down the runway. I was on a fairly low altitude flight profile so I had 2 external drop tanks but the take-off was smooth and the full moon that was about to disappear into the western sea gave plenty of light after clearing the end of the runway. Back under the hood on my climb out, I settled down to the lonely routine of flying the aircraft and those two demanding needles on the Radist panel. At 5 minutes before time zero, I jettisoned both tanks. I had set my altimeter a little on the high side so that when the tanks left the aircraft the "position error" in the altimeter would be correct for the "clean aircraft" configuration. On this flight, I was positioned short of the bomb at time of detonating so that I would get frontal heat to see what effect it would have on the engine intake flow and then I would receive the shock wave while directly above the bomb and fireball. It was a pretty dicey position and I had to be precisely positioned to get the "shock wave" and not the fireball, which would be rising rapidly behind it.

When I started throwing the instrumentation switches at 20

seconds to go, I felt convinced that the shot was going to "fire." 5-4-2-camera switch "on" -2-goggle "down" 1 "0." Hands over my eyes with a last-minute glance at the attitude indicator to be sure I was flying straight and level. Then it came again. The brilliant white flash of light that was really painful to my eyes and then without trying, I could see all of the bones in my hand. I was closing my eyes as hard as I could but it didn't help. In a few seconds, the darkness returned until I took my hand away and even before I could take off my lightproof goggles, I could tell the light was fading away. Pushing the goggles up away from my eyes was another shock that I never could adjust to and that was the fact that when I took my hand from in front of my goggles everything was black but as I pulled the goggles up away from my face my cockpit was still almost blindingly filled with the fading white light. This was also eye-hurting brightness but as I squinted, I could see the light rapidly fading, leaving behind the ultraviolet light that penetrated the skin of the aircraft. As it faded the ribs and stringers, which made up the heavier structure of the airframe around the cockpit casts darker shadows before the ultraviolet faded completely.

I had a very bright floodlight mounted over the instrument panel for lighting so that the movie camera installed over my right shoulder on the ejection seat rail could record the instruments. Suddenly that was all the light left and as my eyes started to focus again, I saw that my right wing had started to drop slightly causing me to be 1 degree off heading. My altitude was still right on and my progress needle was on target. The course needle was a hair off to the left but still inside the center circle requiring me to do very little to center it.

Now I had to get back to flying those gauges and when I checked *my time from "time zero" it was rapidly approaching the time for the shock wave to hit. Then it hit! There is no way to describe what it is like to feel that crash against my spine. It was extremely painful and not the type that goes away immediately. It goes all the way up the spine to the back of the neck and creates an immediate headache. My eyes were so jarred that they refused to focus for several seconds and then I could only concentrate on one instrument, the attitude indicator. The whole instrument panel was a blur (and verified when the movie films were reviewed) for several seconds but my reflexes automatically had me reaching the hood snap releases and unzipping it as quickly as I could. When I pulled it back, I was closer to the rising fireball than I had previously been (because of my being directly overhead at the time of the shock wave arrival) and this was an indescribably awesome spectacle!*

My attention was drawn back to my engine instruments. It seems that after flying critical test missions where every instrument can become essential to the data you acquire a sixth sense that tells you when something moves that shouldn't. That is what happened in this case as I caught a glimpse of my tailpipe temperature needle fluctuating. Checking all of the other engine instrument readings there was no fluctuations that would relate to the fluctuations of the tailpipe temperature so I had to assume the shock wave impact had damaged the needle attachment. It was a critical position that left me no place to go if an engine or airframe failure occurred. I was too close to the bomb danger area to bailout and too far from any rescue aircraft or ships. I always knew that on any of these shots, if the aircraft was damaged to the extent that it wouldn't stay in the air, there was little chance for me to be rescued.

The danger area from the shots varied with the yield of the bomb but all of the hydrogen bombs were of a magnitude that the contamination area was well outside of gliding range. The long flight back was uneventful but I felt that the bird wasn't flying as smoothly as it should, and after landing, I discovered why. The tailpipe brackets holding it to the aft part of the fuselage were completely broken and the rear portion of the pipe was just floating. One of the forward three brackets was completely broken loose. My tailpipe temperature gauge was indicating properly. In addition to these failures, both landing flaps were buckled and seared. Lower fuselage seared with several large buckled places, horizontal stabilator buckled and seared, fuselage light melted, wing to fuselage fairings seared and buckled and the camerabubble was blistered. My back and both hips hurt so bad that I had difficulty getting out of the cockpit.

Monday June 25: *"Rip" Collins with the Hollywood picture agency offered Kitch and me a flight to Tarawa tomorrow. Kitch and I celebrated at the club with a couple of drinks that I shouldn't have had. When we got back to the room the bottle of Ballantine scotch that Joe Bourgorno had given me had been consumed by Robbie, John and Mitchell. I had given it to them stating that I wasn't supposed to be drinking. They kept us up most of the night celebrating something. I was never quite sure just what that was. Rip came in to say the Tarawa trip was cancelled and our engineers came in to tell me the shot was bigger than predicted and they were happy with my data. They should be and my poor back and hips would like to have been instrumented to show them how it really felt to get that "good" data. Maintenance says my aircraft has more damage than they first thought and will take longer to fix.*

Operation Redwing: Dakota

Operation Redwing: Lacrosse

Operation Redwing: Mohawk

Operation Redwing: Zuni

Operation Redwing: Cherokee

Runway at Eniwetok

INDIVIDUAL FLIGHT RECORD (PILOT)

1. MONTH AND YEAR: MARCH 1956 — 2. SHEET NO.: 105
3. AF OR COMMAND: WADC — 4. WING, GROUP, AND SQUADRON OR UNIT: TEST AIRCRAFT UNIT, TASK GROUP 7.4
5. LAST NAME—FIRST NAME—MIDDLE NAME: EVANS, NORVIN C JR
6. BASE AND LOCATION: ENIWETOK ATOLL, M.I. APO 187, San Francisco, Calif — 7. DUTY AFSC: 8744
8. ORIGINAL RATING AND DATE: Plt 1 Feb 45 — 9. PRESENT RATING AND DATE: Sr Plt 27 Feb 53 — 10. ☐ WHITE ☒ GREEN ☐ NO INST. CERT. DATE OF EXPIRATION: 10 September 1956
11. DATE OF BIRTH (Day, month, year): 10 September 1924 — 12. SERVICE NO.: A0937553 — 13. GRADE AND COMPONENT: Captain (AFRes)
14. TYPED NAME AND GRADE OF OPERATIONS OFFICER (Or authorized deputy): GEORGE M KHOURY CAPTAIN USAF
15. SIGNATURE (On original and duplicate copies): [signature]

SECTION I

DAY OF MONTH (A)	AIRCRAFT TYPE, MODEL, SERIES (B)	AUTH MISSION SYM (C)	COMMAND AND/OR RADIO CONTROL PILOT TIME (D)	NO. LANDINGS (E)	AIRCRAFT COMMANDER TIME (F)	INSTRUCTOR PILOT TIME (G)	FIRST PILOT TIME (H)	DAY VFR (I)	DAY WEATHER INSTRUMENT (J)	NIGHT VFR (K)	NIGHT WEATHER INSTRUMENT (L)	HOOD (M)	COPILOT (N)	COPILOT DAY VFR (O)	COPILOT DAY WEATHER INSTRUMENT (P)	COPILOT NIGHT VFR (Q)
February time not previously recorded																
28	JF-94C	X-1		1			0:30	0:30								
28	JF-86N	X-2		1			1:45	1:45								
29	JF-100	X-1		2			3:00	3:00								
March																
1	JF-100	X-1		1			1:30	1:30								
1	JF-94C	X-1		1			0:40	0:40								
1	JF-86F	X-1		1			0:50	0:50								
1	JF-86D	X-3		1			1:00	1:00								
2	JF-86A	X-2		1			1:05	1:05								
26	JF-84F	X-3	ENIWETOK	1			1:05	0:50				0:15				
27	JF-84F	X-1		1			1:15	0:55				0:20				
28	JF-84F	X-1		2			2:40	1:15				1:25				
29	JF-84F	X-1		4			5:05	2:20				2:45				
16. TOTALS THIS SHEET				17			20:25	15:40				4:45				
17. TOTALS BROUGHT FORWARD		SHEET No. 104		705		308:55	2647:35	2355:35	111:30	181:40	3:30	304:15	137:40	127:30	2:10	8:00
18. TOTALS TO DATE				722		308:55	2668:00	2371:15	111:30	181:40	3:30	309:00	137:40	127:30	2:10	8:00

AF FORM 1 AUG 54 5 Previous editions of this form may be used.

March 1956 Flight Log

INDIVIDUAL FLIGHT RECORD (PILOT)

1. MONTH AND YEAR: April 1956 — 2. SHEET NO.: 106
3. AF OR COMMAND: WADC — 4. WING, GROUP, AND SQUADRON OR UNIT: Task Group 7.4, Test Aircraft Unit
5. LAST NAME—FIRST NAME—MIDDLE NAME: EVANS, NORVIN C JR
6. BASE AND LOCATION: APO 187, San Francisco, Calif. — 7. DUTY AFSC: 8744
8. ORIGINAL RATING AND DATE: Plt 1 Feb 45 — 9. PRESENT RATING AND DATE: Sr/Plt. 27 Feb 53 — 10. ☐ WHITE ☒ GREEN ☐ NO INST. CERT. DATE OF EXPIRATION: 10 Sept 1956
11. DATE OF BIRTH (Day, month, year): 10 Sept 1956 — 12. SERVICE NO.: AO-937553 — 13. GRADE AND COMPONENT: Capt. (AFRes)
14. TYPED NAME AND GRADE OF OPERATIONS OFFICER (Or authorized deputy): CHARLES R. ANDERSON, Major, USAF.
15. SIGNATURE (On original and duplicate copies): [signature]

SECTION I

DAY OF MONTH (A)	AIRCRAFT TYPE, MODEL, SERIES (B)	AUTH MISSION SYM (C)	COMMAND AND/OR RADIO CONTROL PILOT TIME (D)	NO. LANDINGS (E)	AIRCRAFT COMMANDER TIME (F)	INSTRUCTOR PILOT TIME (G)	FIRST PILOT TIME (H)	DAY VFR (I)	DAY WEATHER INSTRUMENT (J)	NIGHT VFR (K)	NIGHT WEATHER INSTRUMENT (L)	HOOD (M)	COPILOT (N)	COPILOT DAY VFR (O)	COPILOT DAY WEATHER INSTRUMENT (P)	COPILOT NIGHT VFR (Q)
2	F-84F	X-3		1			:55	:45				:10				
4	F-84F	X-1		1			1:00			1:00						
6	F-84F	X-1		1			:50	:50								
9	F-84F	X-1		1			:50	:40				:10				
9	F-84F	X-3		1			:55	:55								
10	F-84F	X-1		2			2:30	:45				1:45				
11	F-84F	X-1		1			1:30	:30				1:00				
12	F-84F	X-1		1			:25	:25								
21	F-84F	X-3		1			:50	:50								
22	F-84F	X-1		1			1:25	:40	:45							
23	F-84F	X-1		3			3:45	1:40	2:05							
24	F-84F	X-1		1			1:35			:50	:45					
26	F-84F	X-1		1			1:00	:40				:20				
28	F-84F	X-1		1			1:00	:10			:30	:20				
30	F-84F	X-1		1			1:50	:35	1:00			:15				
16. TOTALS THIS SHEET			0	18	0	0	20:20	9:25	3:50	1:50	1:15	4:00	0	0	0	0
17. TOTALS BROUGHT FORWARD		SHEET 105	0	722	0	308:55	2668:00	2371:15	111:30	181:40	3:30	309:00	137:40	127:30	2:10	8:00
18. TOTALS TO DATE			0	740	0	308:55	2688:20	2380:40	115:20	183:30	4:45	313:00	137:40	127:30	2:10	8:00

AF FORM 1 AUG 54 5 Previous editions of this form may be used.

April 1956 Flight Log

May Flight Log 1956 showing Lacrosse and Cherokee missions.

June Flight Log showing Seminole, Flat Head, Osage, Inca and Dakota missions.

INDIVIDUAL FLIGHT RECORD (*PILOT*)

1. MONTH AND YEAR: July 1956
2. SHEET NO.: 109
3. AF OR COMMAND: WADC
4. WING, GROUP, AND SQUADRON OR UNIT: Task Group 7.4, Test Aircraft Unit
5. LAST NAME—FIRST NAME—MIDDLE NAME: EVANS, NORVIN CHARLES JR.
6. BASE AND LOCATION: APO 187, San Francisco, California
7. DUTY AFSC: 8744
8. ORIGINAL RATING AND DATE: Plt. 1 Feb 45
9. PRESENT RATING AND DATE: Sr/Plt. 27 Feb 53
10. ☐ WHITE ☒ GREEN ☐ NO INST. CERT. DATE OF EXPIRATION: 10 Sept 1956
11. DATE OF BIRTH (Day, month, year): 10 Sept 1924
12. SERVICE NO.: AO-937553
13. GRADE AND COMPONENT: Captain (AFRes)
14. TYPED NAME AND GRADE OF OPERATIONS OFFICER (Or authorized deputy): CHARLSS R. ANDERSON, MAJOR, USAF.
15. SIGNATURE (On original and duplicate copies): per James O. Cobb, Colonel, USAF

SECTION I

DAY OF MONTH (A)	AIRCRAFT TYPE & MODEL SERIES (B)	AUTH MISSION SYM (C)	COMMAND AND/OR RADIO CONTROL PILOT TIME (D)	NO. LANDINGS (E)	AIRCRAFT COMMANDER TIME (F)	INSTRUCTOR PILOT TIME (G)	FIRST PILOT TIME (H)	First Pilot Day VFR (I)	First Pilot Day Weather Instrument (J)	First Pilot Night VFR (K)	First Pilot Night Weather Instrument (L)	HOOD (M)	COPILOT (N)	Copilot Day VFR (O)	Copilot Day Weather Instrument (P)	Copilot Night VFR (Q)
2	F-84F	X-1		2			2:40	:15		:20	:25	1:40				
3	F-84F	X-1	Mohawk	1	Mohawk		1:00			:10	:50					
7	F-84F	X-1		2			2:45	:45	:15			1:45				
9	F-84F	X-1	Apache	1			1:40	:40	1:00							
11	F-84F	X-1	Navajo	1			1:30			:30	1:00					
12	CLOSED...RETURNING TO HOME STATION															
16. TOTALS THIS SHEET			0	7	0	0	9:35	1:40	1:15	1:00	2:15	3:25	0	0	0	0
17. TOTALS BROUGHT FORWARD	SHEET NO. 108		0	770	0	308:55	2731:25	2394:00	120:10	189:35	7:15	329:20	141:20	129:40	3:10	8:30
18. TOTALS TO DATE			0	777	0	308:55	2741:00	2395:40	121:25	190:35	9:30	332:45	141:20	129:40	3:10	8:30

AF FORM 5, 1 AUG 54. Previous editions of this form may be used.

July Flight Log showing Mohawk, Apache, and Navajo missions.

"There was an overcast just a little bit above me and the trail left by the rising fireball, as it penetrated the overcast, was one the most fantastic sights I have ever seen. Now you have to believe it was spectacular for me, who was about to burn to death, to become entranced by this pattern of icy ultraviolet Japanese umbrellas exploding outward every thousand feet or so in the wake of the upward rolling fireball which had already disappeared from my view through the overcast. I pushed the control stick to the right and looked for "home plate" which to my pleasant surprise was just where it should have been, some 25 miles away."

NO RELIEF IN SIGHT

My stay on the island was much more stressful than I had been able to describe in my journal because of the lack of productivity during the long times when I had to "stand down." The stomach problem continued and added to my hip pain, which reached a point where my crew had to put my parachute in the seat and then help me up the ladder. The pain was so severe that I would get up with the bomber troops. It took me so long to climb out of bed, take my shower, shave, ride down to the Mess Hall, go to the briefing and get into my aircraft that I needed that extra 2-1/2 hours to get ready for my flights.

Our flight surgeon was literally useless in helping me with either of my health problems and when I could get in to see him he just kept telling me how unfair it was that he was assigned to that miserable place for so long. John, Kitch, and I got to fly on the C-54 to Honolulu. We left at 1300 and landed in Kwajalein for fuel, but when we were ready for take-off, one magneto didn't check out and we had to abort. We went to the club for dinner. At 2230, we were told another C-54 was coming to pick up the cargo. The aircraft was carrying radioactive samples from the shot and was to transfer them to another aircraft in Honolulu that would take them back to the States.

The timing was critical in getting them to their final destination and therefore the other aircraft was dispatched as soon as the problem occurred. At 0430, we were airborne. Kitch, John, and I took turns flying from the copilot's seat and we finally arrived at Hickham Field at 1930 that night. It gave us time to spend one night at the Reef Hotel and then back to the airfield and back to the island. We didn't get any sleep in Hawaii as we took in all the nightclub shows and ended up eating breakfast in the hotel coffee shop just before having to catch the flight back.

My aircraft was out of commission while the damage was being assessed and repaired so I was in no hurry to get back, but the C-54 that we were on was not supposed to be on this trip and the crew had to get back to "Kwag." My hip pain became so severe that I could barely stand up to walk up to the cockpit or go back to the restroom. The canned rations we had on the flight really set my stomach on fire, but when I got back, it took me three painful trips to the dispensary before I could see the flight surgeon. He gave me more Amphajel for my stomach and more APC's for my hip. Neither gave any relief. I was a real physical mess and trying to ignore it was of no help.

My next mission on July 2 was code named "Apache" and it was close to being the last flight I would ever fly. The aircraft had not been ready in time for a functional test flight but I agreed to fly it in the shot without one. John Boughman told me that they had a bad artificial horizon on their ground check so they had just replaced it but hadn't been able to check it out after installing it. I watched carefully during taxi and run up and it seemed to be working as I rotated on lift-off. I noted that the artificial horizon responded properly giving me the normal 15 degree nose up climb attitude.

When I left the shoreline into the inky blackness just after lift-off, I had to fly strictly on that artificial horizon indicator as my primary reference to my aircraft's attitude in relation to the water/ground. There was a sixth sense on that morning that made me feel as though the water was coming up towards me. There was no light anywhere in front or to the side of my F-84 and I was confident that the horizon indicator was functioning properly, but when I looked at my rate of climb on my vertical speed indicator, it showed me in a slight descent. It had to be very slight as I was just above the water when I cleared the shore line on these take-offs and I always held the 15 degree nose high attitude until I had a positive rate of climb and the altimeter (which lags quite a bit behind the rate of climb indication) began to move upward.

Instinctively, I pulled back harder on the control stick and I was sure I could see the white caps almost level with me. That of course couldn't be true otherwise I would have splashed into the black ocean, but I felt as though I was about to. My crew told me after I landed that they were sure I had gone into the water until they saw me zoom upward some distance out from the runway. As I pulled back on the stick, I noted all of the instruments showed me climbing except the artificial horizon, which began indicating a dive. That was all for that instrument and I was now faced with the decision of whether or not I wanted to attempt to fly without my primary flight instrument through the long "under the hood" flight to the exact positioning I had to have or to abort.

I decided to give it a try. I know that anyone who flies unstable fighters of that vintage will tell you that it is a demanding task (disregarding the fact that I was still in the position of having to be as close to the 0.1 of a second at time zero as possible). I settled down to my best concentration mode and went under the hood flying on "needle and ball." To add to my problems the Radist needles were not working and my voice controller was not on station, so I had Floyd Gibbs, the manager, working me. Things were working out pretty good and at 15 seconds to go I started my switching sequences.

Nothing happened at time zero. The countdown had stopped at 7-6-5—but I had to keep my hand on my goggles, ready to pull them down at first indication of light from the detonation and one eye uncovered to keep the needle, ball airspeed, and altitude steady. The next call I got was +10-11-12-13-14 and then, "sorry Bud we must have missed the countdown." Now I was really confused. I knew that the bomb couldn't have gone off, but I was being given the post explosion count and I had to brace myself for the shock wave to arrive. All sorts of things were racing through my mind.

Could Gibbs countdown be one minute off? Is my position off? What has gone wrong? Do I dare open my hood? If the shot was cancelled, why wasn't I called? If I open my hood and it "goes off" it will blind me. What the hell is going on? At 2 minutes past time zero, I got the call that the shot had been delayed and did I have enough fuel for one more pattern? I had dropped my tanks and didn't know if I could make it but

I told them I would try. I was worn out from the ordeal of having to fly "needle and ball" for so long. Before I got very far into the second pattern, "Barrymore" the main mission controller, called to say the shot was cancelled. I opened the hood expecting to relax a little and fly back to Eniwetok visually only to find that I was in the clouds and would have to "needle-ball" it all the way home!

After making a "GCA" approach and landing in a heavy rain shower, I came back to the barracks completely worn out and soaking wet, and not from the rain! I climbed painfully up into my upper bunk and slept until mid-afternoon, when I had to struggle down and drag that left hip with me to the mission debriefing, and next day mission briefing. Col. Cobb kept us all there after the meeting to give us a lecture on "wet runway landings." Ha!

Following the briefing I flew another flight practicing with MSQ. I had worked with them on an earlier small atom bomb test but it was not a critical positioning the way the upcoming shot was to be, so we both needed to gain each other's confidence. I'm sure that the controller would feel bad if he "miss-positioned" me but not nearly as bad as I would. I flew several racetrack holding patterns, each followed by a simulated live drop run and they seemed to be doing an excellent job. The only person who really knew exactly where I was located, at simulated time zero, was the controller, and I didn't think he was going to cause my loss of confidence by telling me we were 1 or 2 seconds off.

According to his figures on the radio, I was 0.0 on the first run and -0.5 seconds on the last. The one redeeming grace about this mission was that I might be able to fly outside of the contamination area if I suffered damage that would cause me to eject. Not much consolation, but at least I would not be facing 230 miles of open ocean to reach my closest landing site. I did nothing in the evening but had some ice cream as the doctor advised. I had laughed when he told me that was something I could eat, as the snack bar had not had any for a long time. I figured the flight surgeon had some stored away in his clinic, but I didn't bother to comment as to where he expected me to get any and, as it turned out, that night it was available again in the snack bar.

The next morning, July 3rd, I went through the same routine as the morning before, except I slept until 0230 and was able to have breakfast, make the briefing, and get into the air on schedule. This morning the instruments all worked and I flew my MSQ mission with Forsey as my controller, as I had on the previous day. This was classified as a mild shot, which meant a considerably smaller bomb would be exploded on the northern end of our atoll. This meant nothing to those of us flying effects aircraft, as our data objective was to acquire as much heat and shock load as the structural design limits of each type aircraft could theoretically survive.

As always, I was the closest to the detonation and because this bomb was under a megaton, I was positioned low and close. I really felt that compared to the Bikini shots this would be a piece of cake! Everything was right on schedule and my radar controller was doing a great job, so I was about as relaxed as one could be flying into an "A" bomb blast. At time zero, I was told I was right on in all aspects and when the blast and flash of light enveloped the cockpit, I had my hand over my eyes in the normal fashion. The brilliance of the light was just as intense as the "H" bombs but only seemed to last for a second or two. I took my hand away from my eyes but didn't push my goggles away because just when I took my hand away the light was still so bright that I had to put my hand back for another second.

Something definitely was not right about this, so after another second or two I took my hand away again and pushed my goggles up away from my eyes. The cockpit was still filled with very, very bright blue-white light of increasing intensity, which had begun to change from white to orange along with the ultraviolet. This definitely was not normal. Instead of fading, the light was getting brighter. What was going on and why was the cockpit getting hotter and hotter? My whole body began to feel as though I was searing over a hot grill but it began to change to extreme heat as though literally millions of long hot needles were stabbing down through my body. All I could think of was the almost fatal mission that I had been forced to abort and that if I hadn't, I would have flown into the fireball.

I suddenly became acutely aware of the smell and sight of smoke rolling into the cockpit from under the instrument panel and a definite glow from fire burning around my flight boots. Time seems to slow considerably when the heart rate and adrenaline begin to go into afterburner. There seemed like an interminable period of time when there was a lot of doubt in my mind as to whether I was frying along with the aircraft or not. I couldn't abort or do anything except wait to see if I started burning, as the shock wave hadn't arrived. I forgot about checking the seconds for arrival, so I was not prepared when it hit. That didn't bother me much as I had far greater problems on my hands to deal with.

As soon as I could take my hand completely away from my eyes, I tried to unsnap the hood. Even through my semi-flame proof gloves, the hood was so hot I couldn't put my fingers on the snaps long enough to pull any of them loose. That lasted perhaps as long as it took me to determine that if I wanted to get out of the aircraft, I would have to open that hood. On the third or fourth try, I managed to painfully unsnap, unzip, and pull the hood partially back. The smoke that poured down from in front of me where the hood had been pulled back blinded me for a second or two. Now I was sure I was on fire because everything I could see in front of me was bright reddish-orange. I tugged on the sides of the hood and managed to get it back about half way. To my great relief I could see a very thin horizon line where the first light of dawn was making its usual post shot appearance.

At least I was not going further into the fireball even though it was obvious I was on fire. It didn't seem to matter that the engine fire warning lights were not on as I had all of the positive indications of being on fire. I looked down at my boots, which I had pulled back off the rudder pedals because they were burning my feet, and now I could clearly see flames burning around the flooring and rudder pedal area. Lots of smoke was still coming from that area and all around my upper body from the canopy area. I tried to make a mayday radio call but all I could hear in my headset was a loud crackling static sound. I pushed the hood back a little farther and burning cloth started falling on my legs. I looked back towards where the fireball had propelled itself upward and even with my present predicament—I was amazed at the sight I was greeted with.

There was an overcast just a little bit above me and the trail left by the rising fireball, as it penetrated the overcast, was one the most fantastic sights I have ever seen. Now you have to believe it was spectacular for me, who was about to burn to death, to become entranced by this pattern of icy ultraviolet Japanese umbrellas exploding outward every thousand feet or so in the wake of the upward rolling fireball which had already disappeared from my view through the overcast. I pushed the control stick to the right and looked for "home plate" which to my pleasant surprise was just where it should have been, some 25 miles away.

By now the static in my headset had subsided somewhat. The smoke intensity and flames under my feet had begun to die out. For the first time in a few long, long, seconds I thought I might have a chance of making it out alive.

I had no idea what the overall condition of my "bird" was, but it responded to my control input so at least I could point it in the direction of "home plate!" I had to fly "the gauges" as the smoke was still so heavy that with the lack of daylight I couldn't see much outside. I tried a "Mayday" call and to my relief I heard a reply from my controller acknowledging it and vectoring me toward the approach end of the runway, before asking what my problems were. I responded that I didn't know the extent of the damage but I had lots of smoke and flames inside the cockpit! They cleared me directly to the airport and by the time I was on my final approach the smoke had subsided enough for me to make the landing. The smell from whatever had been burning was still watering my eyes and I could only partially see just enough to land.

It was no problem for me. It is hard to describe the feeling of relief that comes from being so close to an inescapable life-threatening situation and then realizing you still have a chance of surviving. It happens to people in all types of hazardous professions and to pilots, particularly combat and test pilots, which is what I am most familiar with. You just tell yourself that once you see you can "make it," it's all routine now, but you don't dare relax as you've seen others do, with fatal results. You simply tell yourself you're going to make it and when you pull up to a stop at the ramp, it was all just another routine test mission. Well, not really!

The cause of the fire was determined to be the first and only time an aircraft in flight had been under a cloud when a nuclear bomb was detonated close by. The reflection of the intense heat off of the overcast down on top of the F-84 from the bomb caused the asbestos and aluminum cloth to catch fire. All of the black tape, glare shield forward of the hood and the hydraulic fluid that had leaked out around the rudder pedals on the cockpit floor had created other fires. Even the lens on the over-the-shoulder camera in the cockpit under the protective shield had crystallized. (I still have it in one of my souvenir boxes).

The skins on top of the flaps, stabilator, and ailerons were wrinkled and in some cases burned completely through. For several days following this mission, my whole body experienced some residual tingling, most likely a response to the burning needles that penetrated my body during the period of reflected heat and rays following the bomb's explosion. I was not allowed to find out how much radiation I had gotten on this mission, as on all missions, since the first mission, when I exceeded the six-month allowable radiation dosage. My film cartridge measuring device was collected from me as I came back into the operations office and taken off for processing. That evening, I was invited to Col. Samuels' quarters for a party, but not being able to drink the cocktails, it was not that great of an event for me.

Pic 1: Camera mounted over my right shoulder; Pic 2: Crystallized lens and film cartridge to measure radiation, which no one collected, so apparently it didn't really matter.

The following day was the Fourth of July, but I had all of the fireworks I wanted for a while on the third. It also turned out to be not a very good day for celebrating as my crew and I found out that we had to stay to participate in the last shot. I began to feel as though "they" weren't going to be happy until they destroyed the aircraft and very possibly me along with it. That is just what ended up happening to the aircraft except not on the last shot in the series, but one earlier.

Johnny Apple and I had a meeting that afternoon with the operations people and they gave us what they considered to be sound reasons (in their minds) why I needed to stay for two additional shots. It meant a number of more flights that I would have to make in direct violation of Air Force flying regulations by not having an alternate airport at which to land in the event that Eniwetok Airfield was unusable on my return from Bikini. I was told the regulation had been waived for this exercise but no one was able to produce a copy of that waiver. There was nothing to do but face the reality that I wasn't going to quit flying. I had violated the regulation over 50 times since arriving on the atoll. There was only the feeble attempt to draw the brass' attention to the fact that I was being forced by the test requirements to do so. Kitch didn't attend the meeting. He had grown progressively moody and kept to himself a lot. I guess we are all getting a little "Rock Happy" and I found myself reacting to small annoyances in an excessive manner. Even though I knew better, I still let small things bother me. John and I had dinner with Col. Cobb and he assured us that no decision had been made on our staying for the last two shots. I wasn't convinced and my intuition proved correct.

I had a new flash curtain installed and the damage was repaired. On the next shot, the protective light hood worked fine. The weapon didn't reach its predicted yield but I got all of the same brilliant light, X-ray view of the bones in my hand and ultraviolet shadows from the airframe structure. It was nothing overly impressive compared to the previous shots, but there was certainly no way to classify any of them as being "routine." The data was good but because of the lower yield, my position was not where I received the maximum heat and shock effects. I knew this meant that I would have to stay for at least one more shot. My hip was acting up so much that I'm sure that anyone watching me would have to wonder if the Air Force was that hard up that they were sending cripples out to these tests as expendable pilots. I was certain that I would be rendered unconscious from the back and hip pain should I have to eject out of the aircraft. Watching me struggle to climb in and out of the F-84 would have made a good comic film, but once I was seated in the cockpit, I was able to perform all of the normal pilot duties. Only when I tried to change position while seated did the pain bring tears to my eyes, so I tried not to move much during my 1-1/2 to 2-1/4 hour flights.

On July 11, I flew my last mission on Operation Redwing, although it was not scheduled to be the last. Everything was routine and I felt that we would not have a full "go" as this was only a few days after the last shot. I carried two drop tanks because I had to fly the entire pattern out to Bikini at a lower altitude to put me as close to a critical position as the engineers felt they dared. This hydrogen bomb was as close to a "stock pile" weapon as could be predicted and they believed that their prediction of the yield would be very accurate. At five minutes to go, I dropped my tanks, which is always an interesting experience when flying under the hood to such tight tolerances as the attitude, altitude and airspeed all change the second the tanks are blown off the wing by the ejection cartridges. I began to think this might actually be a live mission.

This time the flash and eye pain were so unbelievable that it took longer to get my eyes to focus on the instrument panel. As I was counting down the time on the shock wave clock, the impact of the shock wave arrived well ahead of the expected time and was so violent I felt as though I had hit another aircraft! Now this time the pain in my hip and back actually blinded me for 6 or 7 seconds. That's a long time when you can't tell if you are upside down or what the aircraft is doing following such a tremendous impact. In fact, I had serious concerns as to whether or not I had a "whole" aircraft under my control. The fact that the shock wave arrived so much earlier than predicted was indisputable evidence to me that the bomb had been well over the predicted yield. That is based on the shock wave traveling at the speed of sound and the distance from ground zero I should be if the weapon is as big as the predicted yield. The higher the yield, the further out from ground zero the shock wave propagates and begins traveling towards my retreating F-84F.

With that knowledge, they are able to predict the time it should take for the impact to reach my aircraft. I knew from several indicators: intensity of the light flash, time that it took for the shock wave to arrive, and the force of the impact that this bomb had to have been much bigger than the "swag" predicted by the nuclear "egg heads." Gradually the tears were wiped away with my gloved hand enough to gain control of my wounded, wallowing, steel steed.

Although the fireball was boiling up through 25 to 30,000 feet when I pulled back the flash curtain, the trail it left behind was an unbelievable extravaganza of ultraviolet, still spreading out in ice crystal layers. I started my 140-degree turn to the west back towards Eniwetok and noted that the controls felt a little different. Checking all of my engine instruments, everything was in the green. Something kept bugging me in the way the aircraft was handling, but I was having to deal with my pain and it was still too dark to see much as the afterglow from the bomb had pretty much all faded away. Setting my course and climb altitude, I checked in with "Barrymore" control and advised them that I was still in the air. They gave me my heading to home plate.

In ten minutes or so, the sun began to creep above the horizon behind me. When I looked out, first at my left wing and then the right wing, I had to make a double take to convince me my eyes weren't still out of focus. Carefully surveying the right wing, I could see two very distinct creases from the leading edge of the wing running all that way to the trailing edge. One was about one-third of the way out from the fuselage and the other was about two-thirds of the way out towards the wing tip. I had no doubt in my mind that I was seeing those ridges but really didn't know how badly damaged the wing actually was. The light was still very low and the shadow effect could be giving me an exaggerated picture of the depth of the creases. I decided to carefully move the ailerons from side to side to check the rigidity of the wing and instantly I froze my movement of the stick. The wing not only wiggled from the outboard section but also from the inboard section between the two ridges. It gave me a strong indication that the only thing holding the wing together was the thin outer skin.

I had no idea of what the underside of the wing looked like. I called "Barrymore" for information on the weather back at Eniwetok but they weren't able to help. I certainly didn't want to fly into any bumpy weather. I also asked if they could vector Kitchens towards me so that he could check my whole aircraft over from the air. They told me that Kitch had a problem before the shot and had returned to Eniwetok and had landed. I slowly climbed to 35,000 feet to hopefully fly above any cloud build-ups and out of any turbulence. The F-84F, like all high-performance fighter aircraft, has a rigid wing that is built to have very little flex. The hydrogen bomb shot named "Navajo" had restructured or de-structured the right wing. When I approached the small atoll, I had avoided any rough air and now I was faced with another big decision. I called the control tower at Eniwetok and alerted them to the fact that I had a possible structural problem and would appreciate them alerting air sea rescue SA-16 and crash boats in case I had to eject. I told them that I intended to lower my landing gear at about 15,000 feet and the force of the main landing gear hitting the down stops on the main wing spar could cause my right wing to fold. If that happened I could only hope that it wouldn't hit my canopy if it did fold as that could prevent me from getting out of the cockpit.

I slowed to 160 knots and pulled the circuit breakers to the landing gear system. I felt that if I extended the landing gear with the emergency system it would not hit the stops with as much force as using the normal hydraulic system would. There is one thing about being out in the middle of the Pacific Ocean; there is no one to ask for advice on your aircraft systems so you had better know them. I pulled the emergency gear lowering control cable and the main gear thumped to the down position. The aircraft yawed sharply to the right and then to the left and my heart stopped until I realized that the wing had stayed in place. I took one more look at the right wing, made a slow circling descent down to a very soft no flap touchdown on a welcome piece of hard coral real estate in that huge ocean. I braked carefully to an uneventful stop. I did not chance putting any flaps down to avoid any more loads on the wing. I pulled just off to the side of the end of the runway, shut down the engine, and waited for my decontamination crew to arrive and do their thing. When my troops towed me back to the ramp and put the ladder up to my cockpit, I climbed painfully out of the bird for the last time and limped around to look at my plane's sick wing. It was obvious that we had sustained major damage. I headed for the debriefing office and then to the barracks to pack for home.

That evening at about 1900 hours, John and I received word that we were to leave for home on the next flight out. Poor Kitch's abort forced him to stay for the last shot that I would also be flying in had I not suffered the damage. I never did learn to play the big ukulele and had given it to Brownie. Kitch came in well-oiled and took a personal dislike to Brownie's attempt at music. He grabbed that poor instrument and shattered it against the end of our bunk. It broke up into a million pieces and that broke up all of us into gales of laughter. I really hated to leave Kitch behind as we had suffered through those five plus months together, but as it turned out he was only there for another ten days. I left knowing that the test had been a complete success as far as my participation was concerned. There could not have been any better data than I gave them on my last mission. The structural limits had certainly been well defined as to the size nuclear bomb an F-84F could withstand in dynamic flight. I have paid dearly for that series of tests and as I get older, the effects continue to plague me.

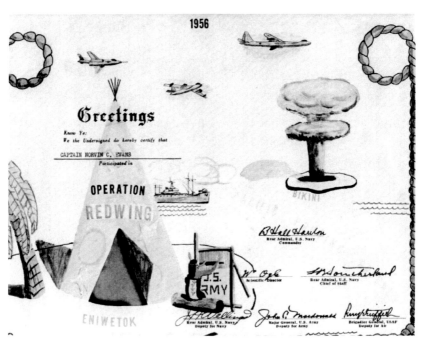

Certificate of Participation in Operation Redwing

I don't know whether or not I will ever go back to those islands again but I know that if I do, it won't be under the same conditions. Having been prevented by security from talking about the project it made the frustration and terrible living conditions that took close to six months to accomplish seven test missions, a faded memory (until I dug out my diary a few months ago). Major Ralph Robinett, Major Charles Anderson, Major Charles Gilmore, Major John Apple, Capt. Ed Little, Capt. Tom Sumner, Capt. Eugene Dietrich, Capt. Willard Mitchell, Capt. Charles Kitchen, 1st Lt. George Lewis, and Yours Truly took close to six months out of our lives, away from our families, out of the main stream of our profession to conduct the most hazardous and demanding flight-testing that anyone could ever imagine. Yet because of its highly classified nature it would mean absolutely nothing in our careers. The details of our participation were so classified that we were not allowed to discuss it with our fellow pilots or our families. My wife, Evie passed away before the information about our tests became public knowledge and so she never really knew why that part of our lives had been taken away from our time together.

After I returned to work at Wright-Patterson, the pain in my hip was added to by pain and swelling in my left hand, elbow, and knee. The pain was so severe that it almost caused an accident on take-off. I was flying an old F-94B with a flight test engineer in the rear cockpit. The aircraft had an instrumentation wire bundle on the outside of the throttle quadrant in the cockpit. In order to light the afterburner it required that the pilot push the throttle outboard towards the bundle. As soon as I released the brakes and started my take-off roll, I pushed the throttle outboard and my fingers on my left hand were squeezed between the throttle and the bundle. The pain was so severe that my eyes became covered with tears, blinding me. All I could do was try to hold my feet equally on the rudder pedals, pull back on the stick and let the aircraft tell me when it was ready to fly. About the time the wheels left the ground, I began to get a little blurred vision back and continued the mission. As soon as I landed, I reported to the flight surgeon at the hospital and was immediately admitted. I was diagnosed as having acute rheumatoid arthritis and was in the hospital for about two weeks undergoing intensive treatments with Butazoladine. It did the trick but required that I have blood tests every day, so the next month kept me in quarters at home, except when I reported to the hospital for blood tests each day.

Capt. Mel Apt, my classmate at the test pilot school who was assigned to Fighter Test at Edwards AFB, came through Dayton after a flight evaluation of new European Fighters. He stayed at our house while being debriefed by Air Intelligence. I received a call for him while I was at work. I relayed the message when Mel came by the flight line to tell him he had to get back to Edwards that night so that he could get his flight in the X-2 Rocket Research Aircraft. I was anxious to hear from him following the flight as he promised he would give me a full account after he landed. Instead, I received a call from a friend at Edwards telling me that Mel had been killed. He had flown the aircraft on such a perfect profile that the aircraft had exceeded the speed it was supposed to reach. In so doing, it passed the point at which it could maintain directional control and had begun to tumble, eventually falling into a flat spin.

"Five months after arriving at Edwards, I had major surgery for a malignant melanoma cancer, which kept me in the hospital outside of San Francisco for five and one-half months and grounded me for 14 months."

OFF TO EDWARDS

Shortly after Mel's accident I was transferred to the Fighter Test Section at Edwards AFB, thus starting a seven-year assignment that was beyond belief from a test pilot's view. Five months after arriving at Edwards, I had major surgery for a malignant melanoma cancer, which kept me in the hospital outside of San Francisco for five and one-half months and grounded me for 14 months.

Kitchens left the Air Force to go to work for Lockheed and became the Chief F-104 Test Pilot. I saw a lot of him and Wanda, his wife, socially. I flew chase for him, and flew test flights out of his office on the F-104's at Palmdale, California. As I noted earlier, I was the last person to see him alive on that fateful late night take-off in his old twin engine Lockheed "12" on his way to Las Vegas. I lost contact with Johnny Apple after he left Wright-Patterson and learned that he lives about

120 miles from me here in Florida. I heard that Robinett went to work for Saudia Airlines after he retired. Chuck Anderson went to work for General Electric after retiring and flew with airlines all over the world, checking operation procedures on the G.E. engines. I saw him regularly at the Society of Experimental Test Pilot Symposiums all over the U.S. and Europe. Tom Sumner was assigned to the Space and Missile Systems office in Los Angeles when I was working for Sundstrand and Northrop. We lived in the same apartment building and I saw him occasionally. He moved to Hawaii and I have seen him a couple of times in Dayton at our "Wright-Stuff Reunions" which were held every two years.

Gilmore was assigned to Bomber Test at Edwards for a few years while I was there. He stayed in the area after retiring from the Air Force and died suddenly from cancer. Dietrich is living in the Washington, D.C. area and was President of the Washington Aviation Club in Crystal City. I heard Ed Little became Vice-President of Air Bahamas Airlines. I have not heard of Willard Mitchell for a number of years and have no idea what has happened with him. Bob Mercer went to work for NASA in Houston, Texas and I saw him a lot in the 60's and 70's. You might have expected at least one of the dedicated officers who were performing such high-risk flight-testing for our Air Force would have made General but the only one who did was the pilot who dropped the F-101 in on landing at Dayton, thus avoiding having to go on the tests.

RETURN TO EDWARDS

Following my release from the flight surgeon, I returned to duty, flew several flights in test aircraft, and then flew a VC-47 to Kansas to Mel Apt's funeral. In mid-October 1956, I received my official orders assigning me to Fighter Test Operations at the Air Force Flight Test Center, Edwards Air Force Base, California. I had to sell our house near Wright-Patterson, clear the base, and pack the family for our trip out west to the desert. I was lucky and sold the house to the first person to look at it. He was a test pilot from the Bomber Test Operations section and I was happy to get $1,000 more than I paid for it. Of course, I had made a lot of improvements, but we felt lucky that we did not have the burden of that mortgage hanging over our heads while we were on the other side of the country.

Our trip to Edwards was uneventful and when we arrived, it was quite a different type of reception than when we arrived for the school. The Wherry Housing area was fairly nice and we thought the three bedroom houses were great. Our assigned house was not ready, but Major Robert Stevens, "The Silver Fox," was leaving on temporary duty for a few weeks, and his wife, Joy, was visiting her home in Texas, so he offered us his house until ours was ready. What a difference from the treatment we received as a student. We settled into base living and I into fighters, where I was accepted as part of the test pilot family.

There was a little thing that always accompanies the new guy in any flying organization and particularly with fighter pilots. You have to prove yourself to everyone. It's different in cargo and bombers where they can assign you to a test program but there is usually someone flying with you either in the co-pilot seat or in the pilot seat to watch while you are conducting the tests. In the single seat fighter, the only way you can be evaluated as to how well you do your job is your data, which the engineers evaluate and the chase pilot's observation (if you are on a hazardous test and are required to have one).

In November, my first month, I flew 40 flights and 46 hours. Most of the flying was in the F-86F, F-84F, and F-100A, delivering steel bombs in the "toss" and "over-the-shoulder" release maneuvers used for nuclear bombs. The Air Force had thousands of 250, 500, and 1,000-pound steel bombs but very few nuclear shapes that the tactical and strategic fighter units could use for practice drops. Our project was to determine the comparative flight profile of the steel bombs, relative to the same flight patterns used to deliver the nuclear shapes. The plots were made from the Ascania tracking cameras after hundreds of deliveries were made with these three types of aircraft at varying release angles and speeds. The engineers were able to provide the using commands with graphs showing where the nuclear shape would have hit relative to where the steel bomb actually hit. This allowed them to set up their targets to represent the location of the nuclear target while actually delivering the steel bomb.

The flying was not actually the most sophisticated flight testing, but the 560 knots run-in as low to the ground as possible and the constant 4 "g" pull-up's while keeping your wings perfectly level so as to prevent any azimuth error out of the bombs trajectory required a lot of pilot concentration. The operational units were to have special bomb delivery systems installed but our drop aircraft had the standard gun sights, so the effort was strictly pilot feel as to angle and direction once you pointed the nose at the target and started the pull-up.

As I said, it was fun but not the normal flight-testing I was expecting. It didn't take long however until I was taking part in the Phase VI tests of the F-86H and F-100D and Phase IV on the F-104A and TF-102A. At that time, flight-testing was divided into phases instead of the category system that was later adopted. Phase "I" was the first flights on a newly designed aircraft and was conducted strictly by the contractor to determine the basic flight capability of the aircraft and to correct any serious flight or system problems before giving it to the Air Force for evaluation. Phase II was the portion of flight testing where the test pilots at Edwards flew the aircraft throughout its speed and maneuvering range and gave it back to the contractor with their evaluation as to how well it met the Air Force specifications. Phase III was the portion of the test program where the contractor made the changes in the aircraft recommended by the Air Force in Phase II and their pilots evaluated those changes. Phase IV was the portion of the testing process whereby the Air Force received two of the newest aircraft and conducted a complete performance and stability and control flight test program throughout the designed flight regime. Phase V was the all-weather and environmental testing conducted by Wright-Patterson, and Phase VII was the portion of testing conducted at Eglin AFB, Florida where the weapon system for the new model aircraft was tested. Phase VI was conducted at Edwards with 4 to 6 of the first production models of the new aircraft and the machines were flown as close to an operational profile as possible. The using command (the Tactical Air Command, the Air Defense Command, the Strategic Air Command, etc.) sent pilots, armorers, and maintenance personnel to participate in the evaluation of the aircraft's ability to perform the operational tasks required by the using command.

One of the other jobs we had was flying safety chase for any hazardous test flights flown by military or civilian test pilots. These flights were "high responsibility" assignments and they required all of your attention being directed towards the test aircraft and no opportunity to look at your own aircraft's engine instruments. We were chasing everything from F-104, B-45, DD-558, X-1E, DC-8, Convair 880, A-5D, A-4D, F-101A, etc. Our responsibility was to immediately report anything unusual occurring on the test aircraft to the test pilot or in the case of a critical failure, to call the ground test radio describing what was happening to the test aircraft and pilot.

In January 1957, I was assigned to fly the Phase IV performance flight test program on the F-101A. This was my first test project at Edwards and I was delighted with the idea of finally getting the chance to fully apply the principles of flight-testing that I had worked so hard to learn in the Test

Pilot School. Not that a lot of the basic principles of flight aerodynamics taught in the school hadn't been used in most of the flight-testing I had performed thus far. I had participated in performance, stability, and control test flights on other pilot programs since my being assigned to Edwards, but this was to be my program as the primary test pilot. I had been back at the Flight Test Center for only a little over three months and this assignment meant that I was accepted as being a full-fledged test pilot by my bosses at Edwards. They were Col. Horace Hanes, the Director of Flight Test, Lt. Col. Danny Grubaugh, Chief of Flight Test Operations, and Major Stu Childs, Chief of Fighter Operations.

In March of 1957, I flew an F-80 to Andrews AFB in Washington, DC to attend the funeral of one of our test pilots and on returning to Edwards, Evie noticed that I had a large blood stain on the back of my flying suit's right leg. She looked at the back of my right thigh and said I had a black mole that had been bleeding. I was scheduled to have a special physical exam the next afternoon prior to going back to Wright Field to be fitted for a pressure suit. When I showed the mole to the Flight Surgeon, he called in the Chief Surgeon, who was my next-door neighbor. He examined it and after a private discussion with the Flight Surgeon and a couple of phone calls, he looked at me with a grave expression and said, "Bud, if that was on my leg, I would have it removed this afternoon but as the operating room is closed and all of the surgical staff have left for the day, I want you here at 0630 tomorrow morning and plan on staying for 2 or 3 days in the hospital."

I protested that I was scheduled on a flight to Dayton the next morning but he told me that those plans would have to be changed. I was on the operating table by 0700 the next morning and while I was still being sewed up, the surgeon ordered the large ball of tissue removed from my right rear thigh to be bottled and shipped directly to Parks Air Force General Hospital in Livermore, California. I spent one night in the hospital and then in two days left for Dayton and the altitude test chamber at the Wright Field labs for my 100,000 foot altitude ride. I had almost forgotten about the mole as I began flying my first performance test flights in the F-101A.

About three weeks after the operation, I came home after work and found my neighbor, the surgeon, sitting at my kitchen table sipping a martini with Evie. It wasn't unusual as all of us at the remote base in the Mojave Desert were close friends and neighbors were often dropping by after work to chat. I told Evie to make one for me and I went to the bedroom to change out of my flight suit.

I came back to the kitchen and sat down. I asked how things were up at the hospital. I was just making the usual casual talk and having no particular subject in mind. The doctor told me that the biopsy came back on my mole and it was malignant! It didn't sink in as to the seriousness of the report, as I thought it was just a skin cancer and I knew most of them could be cured. I was in no pain and had no after effects from the surgery. There were no physical restrictions in my flying since the surgery and I was feeling great. He said he had made an appointment for me at 1300 the next day with the Tumor Board's Chief Surgeon at Parks General Hospital up near San Francisco. It was on the Friday before the Easter weekend and we had plans to go to Las Vegas, Nevada with a group from Flight Test Operations for the weekend, and that meant I would not get back to Edwards until later Friday afternoon. That also meant we wouldn't arrive at Vegas until very late. We were taking the girls as some of the casinos had big Easter egg hunts for the children on Sunday morning and Tracy and Kerry were all excited about sharing the hunt with their friends. At first, they were afraid that the Easter Bunny wouldn't know where to leave their eggs and gifts when they were away from home, but they had been convinced that he left even more eggs in Las Vegas and that had done the trick.

"...the Tumor Board Secretary looked at me and asked me what I wanted. I told her who I was and that I had an appointment with Doctor Gathright. She gave me the most pathetic look when she said in a shaken voice, 'You are Captain Evans?' I felt that the look she gave me was one of looking at a condemned man..."

THE REST OF THE STORY

I made a couple of calls and arranged to fly to Hayward Airport on the east side of the San Francisco Bay. Parks was located about 15 miles to the east of Hayward and the hospital agreed to have a staff car meet me. Tom Armstrong, one of the fighter section test pilots, was working on a super-secret project (the U-2) up near Indian Springs, Nevada and I knew he was flying a T-33 north on Friday morning. He dropped me off at 1100 and was going to pick me up on his flight back to Edwards that afternoon. He was also going to Las Vegas and taking his children, so I figured I had solved that problem.

A hospital staff car picked me up at the Hayward Airport and delivered me to the old tar paper World War II Navy Hospital that had been turned over to the Air Force. It was made up of a number of one-story barracks type buildings connected by covered passageways. I was early and went to the dining hall for a bite of lunch. I was wearing my tan bloused uniform that had my combat ribbons on it. When I walked into the Tumor Board office where I had been ordered to report, the Tumor Board Secretary looked at me and asked me what I wanted. I told her who I was and that I had an appointment with Doctor Gathright. She gave me the most pathetic look when she said in a shaken voice, "You are Captain Evans?" I felt that the look she gave me was one of looking at a condemned man. That was my first clue as to the seriousness of melanoma cancer but I felt great and was convinced that there wasn't anything seriously wrong with me.

When I sat down and listened to what the doctor had to say I was suddenly aware as to why she gave me that "death stare." He said that he could see that I had been exposed to life threatening situations and knew that I was married so he wasn't going to hold anything back as he figured I could handle the hard truth. He told me that I had the quickest and most deadly cancer there was. If after they conducted a number of tests on me, they found any signs that the cancer had spread to any part of my body he would not subject me to painful surgery, as there was nothing they could do to prevent me from dying. That "if" they (the Tumor Board) decided to operate on me, my chances of survival were not good. The fact that the Edwards doctor had sent the tissue in for biopsy when he did was in my favor. He also said that if I had been diagnosed a month earlier they would have done a quarter section on me (removed by right leg at the hip).

A new procedure had just been discovered where they performed a radical lymphadenectomy, removing all of the lymph glands that were downstream from the area of the mole. They had found that the cancer cells travel through the lymph fluid in the body and are trapped in the lymph glands. These glands are there to filter any impurities or infection carried to them by the lymph fluid. The glands feed any infection or abnormal agents slowly into the blood stream where the corpuscles do their thing and carry it off and out of the body. The problem with the cancer cells is they become trapped in the glands and as they multiply, they form a tumor. As it grows, the cancer cells pass into the blood stream and then can travel to any of the organs in the body (that is my layman's over simplification). The only hope is that by removing all of the glands that would be downstream of the cancerous mole they have a remote chance of catching the tumors before they pass the cells into the blood stream. He told me that they would spend several days testing for any sign of spread and if they couldn't find any signs of cancer, they would decide whether to operate on me or not. It certainly changed my understanding of what I was facing and it wasn't something I had any control over.

I told the doctor that I would be back the first thing on Monday morning and that I would at least have a good weekend with my family, but he shot that plan down before I had time to think. He said he was going to put me in a wheelchair and did not want me to walk any more than I absolutely had to. When I protested the cancelling of my Las Vegas plans, he said that if I was alive in five years he would know he had done the right thing but if he allowed me to walk and thus possibly massage any tumor that might have formed, into the blood stream, then he would feel he had not done everything in his power to save me. I had no argument and so I spent the next six days undergoing the series of painful tests wheeling myself around in a wheelchair while feeling perfectly fine. I couldn't believe it when I found myself hoping they would decide to operate on me but knowing the options, it was the only one that would give me a chance of living.

It was a whole new experience to be feeling so healthy and knowing that there was something happening inside you that was killing you. I had faced death literally thousands of times (well maybe hundreds) but I knew if it happened it would be over in seconds or minutes. It was different when you are doing nothing but waiting and thinking about the possibility that you are going to die, but maybe not for a month or even six months. I would have to start waiting for the first signs of something happening inside my body that would give me the first clue as to where it was. I couldn't let myself dwell on it or give in to that type of negative thinking. During the next few days I was probed countless times, filled with colored dyes, had needles stuck into my liver and a chunk taken out without anesthetics, fluoroscoped, and x-rayed, etc.

When I reported before the Tumor Board on the next Thursday, they said that they did not find any positive signs that the cancer had spread and they were scheduling the operation for the next Monday morning. I couldn't believe that I would ever be happy to hear that I was going to be cut open and made ill when I felt so good, but those words were like music to my ears. I had to take their word that there was something seriously wrong with my body. I had a hard time accepting in my own mind that giving up feeling as good as I did to have them operate on me and face the possibility of spending the rest of my life in a wheelchair was going to be beneficial for me. Crazy world, but I naturally was pleased that they hadn't found any signs of the cancer spreading.

One of the first surgeons to perform the radical lymphadenectomy operation lived in San Francisco and had agreed to act as consulting surgeon on my operation. I called Evie as soon as I found out it was going to be done on Monday and she arrived Sunday. Another Air Force Captain had the same cancer on his shoulder, except his had been burned off and when the mole returned three months later they removed it surgically and found it to be malignant. My doctor told me confidentially that it was not likely that they could save him and it didn't do much for my hopes either. I had talked to enough doctors during the week of testing to know that the Edwards doctors did their jobs properly and got the tissue in for analysis without delay. That made the prognosis for my survival much better. Dr. Gathright explained to me that I might not come out of the operation. If I survived for six weeks, I would have a 20% chance of surviving, six months, I would have a 50% chance, and if I survived a year, I would have a 65% chance, 2 years I would have an 80% chance, and 5 years I would have a 95% chance that they had gotten all of that malignancy. He told me that I would probably never be able to walk again, but at best, I would have to use a crutch or cane the rest of my life. That was secondary at that point and my attitude was, one thing at a time, and the number one item on my agenda was praying for their successfully doing their job.

They prepped me the night before and gave me some tranquilizing medication to make me sleep. They told me that the pill they gave me an hour before going into surgery would knock me out and that I wouldn't even know when I went into the operating room. As they wheeled me through the long corridors, I talked with Evie, who was walking beside the cart. Outside of the operating room, Doctor Gathright met us and told Evie that the operation would take a long time and for her not to expect me out before noon. (It was 0700 at the time.) I commented that I was wide awake and that their tranquilizer hadn't worked and he told me not to worry. Then they wheeled me into the operating room and rolled me off of the cart onto the operating table, with my help. I had never had any kind of anesthesia except gas before but they inserted a needle in my arm and I was really upset that I was aware of everything that was happening and had been told I wouldn't be. I remember a lot of eyes looking down at me above the green facemasks and the bright operating room lights glaring down on me. One of the "green clads" looked down at me and said, "We are ready" and that was the last thing I heard.

Somewhere during the eleven and one-half hour operation, I awoke and saw the doctors and nurses standing around the operating table and talking to each other in concerned and irritated tones. I was fully conscious and when one of the "masks" looked at me, I heard her feminine voice say, "He's awake!" A hand reached up to a tube that was hanging from a suspended bottle above me and removed a clamp and the next moment I was lying in the recovery room looking up at Evie's smiling and worried face. Doctor Gathright was looking over her shoulder and they were both telling me that the operation had gone great and a preliminary look at the 55 lymph glands they had removed showed no obvious signs of spread.

The next 16 days I was in intensive care and was sedated heavily. When I was awake, I was in considerable pain. I had to lie on my back as my right leg was in a cast up to my hip and suspended in the air with weights holding it there.

One morning the corpsman came into my room pushing a rack containing four bags of blood hanging from the top.

He proceeded to insert a needle into my arm and attached the tube to one of the bags. The previous night I had a vivid dream and it came back into my memory! My dream was about them giving me the wrong type blood and so I reacted to what the corpsman was doing by asking him if the "B" on the blood bags indicated that it was type "B" blood. He answered that it was, so I told him I was type "O" blood. As he continued to undo the clamp on the tube I reached up, and using what little strength I had, pulled the needle out of my arm creating a messy flow of blood over my bed and the floor. The corpsman became extremely upset and raced out to find the duty nurse. When she came in she tried to explain to me that the doctor had prescribed the transfusion. When I explained that I was type "O" blood and they were trying to give me type "B," she took the chart from the foot of my bed and indignantly said they had taken blood from me the night before and it was type "B." I let her know that if anyone had taken my blood the night before I would have known and no one had. She left and a few minutes later the blood stand was removed and a new stand with four bags of type "O" blood stood in its place.

Another irony was that later in the day I was listening to the radio speaker that was under my pillow when the San Jose station reported the death of a cancer patient who was given the wrong type blood while undergoing surgery at a San Jose hospital. His name was "Evans!"

The doctor explained that they were going to remove all of the tissue down to the muscle on the whole right leg and that it would look like nothing was there but skin and bone. I knew they would have a lot of skin grafting on that leg and it didn't take me long to find out that they had removed skin from my stomach to use for grafting. I had been opened up by two large incisions across my upper and lower abdomen. They had also opened up my right side above the pelvic bone extending down through the groin to half way down the inside of my right thigh. The area on my stomach where the skin had been stripped was covered with gauze and allowed to weep through the porous openings to form a large scab. The first few days it was very sore and then as it began to heal and form the scab it hurt and itched at the same time. I can only explain that first month after the operation as a living Hell.

Doctor Gathright came in to talk to me and check me several times a day for the first month and filled me in on all of the details of the operation. He told me that they had removed the lymph glands from the aorta down through my right groin. The final biopsy report showed no sign of cancer in any of them. When I asked about what was happening when I awoke for that brief second or two, he told me that the electric skin removal machine for stripping the skin for grafting had broken when they were partially into removing the skin from my stomach. They had to send out to another hospital to get one and all they could get was a manual one. That was one of the reasons that the area where they removed the skin was so painful as they couldn't control the depth of the removal of the skin as thin as they could with the electric machine. He also told me that they had removed samples of tissue from every organ in my body, except the heart, for examination and everything turned out negative.

Lying on your back for three weeks can just about drive anyone up the wall and I was no exception. It was impossible to get comfortable and after a couple of weeks I found myself waiting for the next morphine shot and wanting them to hurry up with it. I can't remember just how many days after the operation it was but I know I was still in intensive care and it was time for my midnight shot. I could hardly wait for the nurse to show up when something inside my head shook my brain and asked what the hell was happening to me. Was I hooked on the morphine and was I an addict to the medication?

If I was becoming one, I had better stop taking it and suffer the pain for the short term rather than give in to the temporary relief of the drug. When the nurse arrived, one of the hardest things I have ever had to do was to tell her I did not want the shot. She actually argued with me and told me it was the doctor's orders, but I insisted and after a few minutes, she left. She came back in 20 minutes with the medical duty officer and I explained to him that I was getting so that the only thing I could think about between shots was when I was going to get the next one. He agreed that if I could live with the pain, I didn't have to have the shot but if the pain got too bad that I could ring the nurse and she would give me the morphine. I suffered pure hell for the next week but I didn't give in and Dr. Gathright was very happy with my stand on getting off the drug.

He had told me all about the operation except he failed to discuss the amount of tissue taken from my right leg and finally the big day arrived when the unveiling of the "stick" was to take place. I was back in a private room and when the group of nurses, doctors, and corpsmen gathered around my bed the cast was removed. I didn't know what to expect except that I was going to be able to roll over on my side for the first time in almost a month. As they opened the cast and took it away from my leg I couldn't believe what I was seeing. It looked like a normal leg that had all of the tissue and skin on it. When I excitedly exclaimed that he hadn't stripped all of the tissue from it, he was surprised that he hadn't told me. With all of the other things about the surgery he had failed to mention that they had decided during the operation to only remove an area the size of the palm of my hand from the back of my right thigh around the area where the mole had originally been removed.

He was encouraged by the fact that I could wiggle my toes and later rotate my ankle but we still had no idea whether or not they had cut the main nerve to my right leg. He had said that they wouldn't be able to tell during the surgery if they cut it as they were going to remove all of the tissue and if they missed the nerve it would just be by luck and not through their skill. I was certain that I had a chance of walking again and as I started the road to recovery, I established a new goal. That was to walk and then go back to flying in my old job at Edwards.

Except for the almost fatal wrong blood incident mentioned earlier in this chapter, my road to recovery was unimpeded. I was determined that I was going to walk and as soon as I was strong enough to get up out of the wheelchair on my own power I started making myself struggle with crutches. The distance from my ward to the physical therapy room was a long way and I struggled for weeks refusing to use the wheelchair and finally dragged myself along those long corridors. I pulled myself along on the handrails that graced all of the halls and corridors.

It had been somewhere around six weeks after my operation and I was beginning to feel human and getting fed-up with my inability to get around the way I had thought I would be able to when a memorable event took place that brightened my whole outlook. I was lonesome for some contact with the flight test group at Edwards and although several of the pilots had come up to visit me while I was still bedridden, I was anxious to hear what was happening back in the desert. I heard from Evie regularly and knew what our friends were doing but I guess I needed to talk directly to someone who was flying. Anyway, I was beginning to feel forgotten. It was ridiculous as the workload in flight test at Edwards was always extremely demanding and my friends didn't have the free time to drive 350 miles each way to come and visit.

Anyway, one Friday afternoon I was surprised by a visitor from the F-104A phase VI flight test program. It was one of the Air Defense Command pilots whom I had met and flown with before coming to the hospital. His name was Jim Lowe and he was the youngest pilot to become an Ace in Korea. He came into the room and had smuggled in a six-pack of beer, which was strictly forbidden. I had finished two of them and he had drunk at least that many when the nurse came in and demanded we get rid of the beer. I guess my answer to her was not what she wanted to hear as I explained that I wasn't on any medication and certainly wasn't going to try to leave the room and therefore I didn't see that drinking a beer or two was going to create any serious problems for anyone. I knew that I was feeling the effects of the alcohol, but I was enjoying having a visitor and being brought up to speed on what was happening down at Edwards. Nothing she could have said would upset me or made me give up sharing the gift with Jim. She left and one of the younger nurses came in and sat down and listened to our conversation. I believe she was somewhat taken by Jim, who was a good-looking young officer.

Dr. Gathright was making his usual last minute rounds before leaving for the weekend and came into the room followed by the older nurse who had told us we couldn't have alcoholic drinks in the hospital. Of course, she was correct but I couldn't see that it was doing any harm and she changed her attitude as soon as the doctor sat down on the bed and suggested that we put the remaining cans under a blanket or some place so they couldn't be seen from the doorway. He was a very understanding person and obviously an excellent surgeon.

I can remember that visit by Jim to this day. His taking the time out from his trip to San Francisco for the weekend to stop by had really helped me to regain my fallen spirits. I did have a slight hangover the next morning but everything seemed to head up hill for me from that point on. I was making myself prove that I could walk normally again and the physical therapy people went overboard helping me, once they saw how determined I was. All of the hospital staff members in my ward were extremely good to me and their professional help couldn't have been better in any hospital.

After about three and one-half months, I was given permission from the doctor to spend the weekend at home. The only problem was that home was 350 miles to the south and I didn't have a car. That problem was solved by Evie and the people in flight test. They arranged for the C-47 that returned the Edwards personnel working at the secret test site in Nevada on Friday afternoon, to come by Hayward Airport and pick me up. One of the nurses in my ward dropped me off at the airport on her way home and I got my first glimpse of the outside world. For the past four months I was not sure I would ever see it again.

There are no words in my limited vocabulary to describe the feeling of freedom I experienced when I left the hospital grounds and rode in the car among the living world outside. I had almost the same feeling when I returned home from Eniwetok, but still different. In both cases, it was like being punished and locked up away from my family and friends—like a criminal in jail when I had not committed a crime. I still had a large drain tube protruding from the right side of my abdomen and could not walk very well but I had no trouble getting on and off that C-47 and had a wonderful reception when we arrived at Edwards. My friends still treated me as though I was only going to be gone for a short time longer.

Actually the doctors and I weren't too sure how long I was going to survive, even though the prognosis was good. It was a great weekend being back in my own home, so to speak, as it still belonged to Uncle Sam. We had all kinds of visitors stop by and even though I was pretty weak, I enjoyed every second. I decided that I was going to drive my little Austin-Healy 3000 sports car back to the hospital, despite Evie's protest that I shouldn't try that long of a drive just yet. She offered to drive me back to Livermore. I allowed her to win out. We took the children with us in the old Cadillac and they stayed in the guesthouse until the next Friday when we all drove back to the desert.

At the end of that weekend, I drove the Austin-Healy back to the hospital and made the drive down to Edwards each Friday night and back on Sunday afternoon. That first Sunday when I drove back, I arrived at the Officer's club at about 6:30 P.M. and stopped for dinner. It was a small club but I found a group in the bar that was having a good time. When they saw me at the bar alone, they invited me to join them. The club was having a hard time getting members to patronize it on Sunday night, so the club officer had just started a new program of serving free martinis from 5 P.M. until 6:30 P.M. to attract customers to come in for Sunday dinner. The group who had been enjoying their free drinks was administrative staff with their wives who lived in housing on the hospital grounds. They were a fun group and for the next six weekends, I joined them at the club when I returned each Sunday night. If I didn't arrive by 6:30 they would order several more martinis than they needed and saved them for me. Before I left the hospital, I had been invited to dinner at each of the group's home and I kept in contact with them for a year or so until they moved the hospital to Travis Air Force Base, 70 or so miles from Livermore.

Meanwhile I was feeling more and more confident that I was going to make a full recovery. Every chance I got, I made myself dance and play golf, walking the course. My limp was hardly noticeable and I was determined that I was going to fly again. I was devastated when I met the Tumor Board at the hospital and was told that I was receiving a 100% disability medical retirement. Air Force regulations made it mandatory for anyone having "malignant melanoma." They couldn't understand my protest to such an offer but then they didn't understand what flying and now flight-testing meant to me. I had several long discussions with Dr. Gathright and then with my new friends in the administration office and finally received special approval to stay on active duty although they could do nothing about my being returned to flight status. When I was released back to duty after five and one-half months in the hospital, I returned to my last assigned duty station at the flight test center.

Dr. Gathright's report as to my prognosis being very good for full recovery held very little weight with the Flight Surgeons office. As soon as I returned to Edwards, I went to Lancaster and passed a Civil Aviation Class II physical (even though I still had a drain in my abdomen). The doctor read Gathright's report and said that as long as I was fully mobile and could perform all of the required body movements in the C.A.A. flight physical, I was, in their eyes capable of performing pilot duties. The Air Force was another story and it took me 14 months from the time I was admitted to the hospital and grounded until I was given the "first ever" waiver to return to flight status after having a malignant melanoma.

During the period that I was back on duty at Edwards and not on flying status, the Center Commander and the Flight Test Director were extremely kind to me by allowing me to be carried on the roster in the same slot I held before going into the hospital. This placed me in the position of going right back to work as an experimental test pilot in fighter test operations if and when I was placed back on flying status. I had a lot of fun assignments during that time. I bought an airplane of my own and kept it in the old test pilot school hanger along with the "Bonanza" of General Marcus Cooper, the Center Commander. A test pilot from the bomber section, John Carlson, also had a "Globe Swift" that was kept in that hangar. We flew from the old South Base runway. During the period after my graduation from the Test Pilot School and my return to Edwards, the new base with large new hangars and offices had been completed along with a 15,000-foot runway. The old South Base was used for such things as cable and net types of barrier tests for stopping aircraft on the runway over-run when brake or other system failures kept them from stopping by the time they had used up all the runway.

I remember letting a nameless friend of mine, and fellow

fighter test pilot, fly my Cessna-195 shortly after I had bought it and we took our children up for a flight. We had a pleasant trip around the Desert Valley and my friend was feeling pretty comfortable with his rediscovering the feel of a light aircraft again. He flew the landing pattern perfectly until he flared for the landing. We settled a little quicker than he expected and the spring leaf landing gear spread out and then recoiled us back into the air. He began easing the control wheel forward, a power up exercise, that only aggravated the situation, and we hopped down the runway like a runaway kangaroo.

Finally, he (and I) decided to try again and we made two more hippity-hoppity excursions down the runway. Now, I was too aware of the pride of my expert pilot friend to do any more than help as inconspicuously as possible when we were running out of runway to get us back into the air and his pride would not let him admit that he hadn't figured a way to keep the machine on the ground. On the fourth approach, he looked at me with a smile of despair and motioned for me to make the landing, which my flights out from Illinois when I picked up my airplane had allowed me to master. I slid smoothly onto the ground and as we shut down the engine in front of the hangar, I looked back expecting to see four frightened children in the back seat. To my surprise, they all said that they wanted my friend to do it some more and my daughter, Tracy, asked why I had to stop all of the fun ride my friend was giving them. He became the hero and I was the villain in the children's eyes.

I was used to making speaking trips around the part of Southern California where our aircraft occasionally created sonic booms outside of our "sonic boom corridor." I spoke to

Rotary Clubs, Chamber of Commerce luncheons and all types of civic groups explaining just what caused the loud explosive noise they heard when one of our aircraft passed through the speed of sound. It was another job that had to be done by a test pilot and my status made me useful in not having to take an active pilot away from his test flights to travel to these meetings. The one thing most of us disliked was to have to take time away from our projects for any reason and especially public appearances where you were treated as some kind of hero.

Most of us thought of ourselves as being so very lucky to be allowed to fill a most prestigious job in all of aviation, that we cared little for the well meaning outside praise. Mostly I guess because we didn't feel anyone really understood what our job required and the Clark Gable image of any hotshot pilot jumping into the cockpit and slapping his chewing gum on the side of the fuselage while waving goodbye to his girlfriend, was all Hollywood. In these talks, I tried to give a little background to my audiences as to the flying experience and engineering knowledge that had to be acquired before being assigned the title of "Experimental Test Pilot." I didn't know if I would ever be back in the cockpit again so it kept my spirits up to talk to these people as though I was still one of the active Edwards Test Pilots.

I was ordered to take a memorable public relations assignment in Hollywood with The Toretta Film Company at the Goldwin Studios. I was placed on TDY for a month, but that was tough because the Air Force "per diem" was not nearly enough to pay for a motel room and meals and I was not getting flight pay. It was with mixed feelings that I reported to the studio.

The person whom I was to contact was the producer. I didn't realize until I had spent a day with him and saw how everyone called him Mr. London and the bigger stars called him John with a tone of respect, just who he was in the movie world. He was really nice to me and was one of the few down to earth, solid people I met during my month's stay. The Air Force would not allow the studio to pick up the cost of my room, but Toretta Productions found a nice hotel on the side of Hollywood Hills that I'm sure they subsidized as the price allowed me money left over for food.

Goldwin Studio was right down in the middle of Hollywood and I was surprised at the way they operated the facility. There were several film companies leasing space at the studio and both television movies and films were being made at the same time on the various stages. Sammy Davis, Jr. was making "Porgy and Bess," Gregory Peck was directing "Pork Chop Ridge," Jack Lemmon, Tony Curtis, and Marilyn Monroe were making "Some Like It Hot," and of course, there was the Loretta Young Show that I was working for as the technical director. It was a weak plot about a test pilot flying a high-altitude rocket powered aircraft and the physiological experience of being alone so far detached from the Earth and other human beings that he suffers from what the author calls "The Break-off" syndrome.

I became very unpopular with the writer who I am sure had been paid a lot of money for his story. One of the first things a technical director does is to take the script and read it, making notations on technical errors. The first day I spent looking over the set, meeting key people and studying the script. That night I took my copy and re-wrote at least one third of the dialog and impossible parts of the plot to make it seem feasible from a technical standpoint. The next morning I sat down with John London, John Newland, the director, the writer, and several other production people. As they went over the script line by line, I made my comments. The writer was really upset and I guess if I had written a story and had talked to psychologists and ignored the pilots about whom the story was about, I would defend it in front of the customer the way he did. However, he did and after a morning of changes and rejections, I went to lunch with London and Newland.

We ate at the Goldwin Commissary and sat at a long table in a back room. It must have been for only the elite (like in the show "Duffy's Tavern Where the Elite Meet to Eat") as only the top stars and studio heads ate there. I was surprised after I sat down to see Gregory Peck walk in with his tray and sit down next to John London, who was sitting next to me. John made certain he introduced me to everyone who walked in and I met people I had heard of and some I'm certain I should have. Tony Curtis and Jack Lemmon sat across from me and it seemed that being introduced by John London, I was accepted without question and everyone was one happy family. For most of the time during my month long stay, Tony Curtis and Jack Lemmon came to lunch with women's make-up as they were shooting the sequences for the movie where they posed as women members of the all-girl band. Gregory Peck was a very interesting person and was up on all of the current world news and asked me some very knowledgeable questions about flying at Edwards and about test flying.

During that first luncheon, John explained to me that writers are the most protective and temperamental group that they have to deal with. He explained that the contract that they have to sign when they buy a story is very restrictive as to the changes the producer can make. I understood but told him that since the studio had asked the Air Force, and specifically Edwards AFB, to provide technical assistance that I was obligated to correct the technical errors that I could see. I also let him know that I found the story to be a fantasy. If anyone should have heard of any sort of "Break-Off" phenomenon related to being alone at high altitude, it would be the fighter test pilot, and I had never heard of any such thing. On my first weekend back home, I checked with some of the "X" aircraft pilots with rocket power and they all agreed that some psychologist had probably done his doctorate thesis on that theory without real pilot data to support his self-proclaimed expertise.

John became the mediator between my changes and the author's pride, and for three more days, we plowed through the script. I won most of the glaring errors, but I didn't want anyone to think that I had anything to do with the final show, even though by the time we finished I could have written the complete script and had it appear logical to anyone with an ounce of aviation interest. There was a lot of work involved in producing a television movie that appeared on screen for only one hour. The full crew worked from 0600 until late at night six days a week during the week-and-a-half of actual shooting. During the first weeks, I was allowed to accompany John, the director, technicians, and actors to the screenings in the cutting room for the 2 previous shows that were still being prepared for airing. I could see then why there was no strong interest in making too many changes in the basic script. The shows were being produced for showing at the rate of one each week and there were three or four shows in various stages of completion at all times. John, I soon realized, was being very

Ralph Meeker, with me, looking at the model of the X2 that was used in the movie "The Break Off," where he played the role of an experimental rocket pilot.

patient with me as to his willingness to accept as many of my changes as he did.

On the second day after I arrived, I was walking out of John's office into the hallway when several actors wearing army fatigues approached me from the office of the producer of "Pork Chop Ridge." I guessed they had been in the army but I could tell from the fake mud and blood stains on their clothing that they were playing parts in the movie. They stopped me and with a challenging tone asked if I thought I had earned all of those medals. I was wearing my uniform with the ribbons representing the combat medals I had earned in Korea and was taken aback by the hostile tone of the question. I merely smiled and said, "Yes, there are times I do feel like I earned them." London had stepped out of his office behind me and I was surprised to hear his voice saying, "Captain Evans, don't pay any attention to those boys, they just wished they were real soldiers and not just actors." Their expressions suddenly changed, when I guess they realized that I was not another extra dressed up in costume for the movie and left without further comment. I turned around to see John wink at me and then say that they seldom see real military people on the set and everyone assumes you are an actor when they see you in uniform.

During that first week, I met most of the key players in the production of the show and sat in on the makeup shootings of some of the shows that were in the final stages of completion. One was the story of a Catholic Sister who was a doctor and wore white instead of black. It was played by Loretta Young and during the lunch break we all walked together from the set down to the commissary. She walked with me and I was really taken by her beautiful complexion and particularly by her bright blue eyes that looked like those of a teenager. She was truly a wonderful actress and played her role as the nun all of the time she was on the set and at lunch. Later in her office, she was a normal person, but still a very charming lady. I saw her during both of the days she was shooting make-up scenes from the hospital show and she dropped by the set several more times while we were shooting the "Break-off."

One day at lunch, she embarrassed me by saying to John London in a clear voice that all at the table could hear, "Why don't you convince Bud to try out for one of our shows? He's much more handsome than most of our stars." I knew of course that she was casting a line of blarney but it was an ego builder even so. A week or so later while going into her office with John, he said that I should consider taking a screen test as Loretta had already approved it in front of our whole lunch table and he could set it up. I thanked him for the indulgent compliment, but my job as a test pilot was the most important thing in my life and if I didn't get back on flying status I might consider his offer. He got a large chuckle out of my obvious rejection of the thought and said I would be smart to stay away from the industry and just be one real person instead of many fake ones. That was sound advice and when we were inside Loretta's office, he said that he had just found someone smart enough to stay out of the glittering lights of stardom. I had a great laugh afterwards knowing that I was not actor material and I'm sure they suspected as much. In "the business," a lot of B.S. goes along with most of the conversations, as easily as the "darlings, and love-you's." There were a few straight, fairly normal people in the group that were on the crew and cast but I will have to say that artistic people are, for the most part, very self-involved. There were those would-be artistic people who adopt a sense of self-inflicted superiority over the rest of the population.

I went out after work with Ralph Meeker one night for dinner and I could see why celebrities have to either "go with the flow" or become recluses. I would never have known him from "Joe Anybody" had I not met him through the movie we were working on, but in Hollywood there are a lot of people who are looking to get ahead by being seen with someone who has "made it." He was swamped with people interrupting his drinking and dinner and he seemed to handle it very well with an air of enjoying their attention. I soon learned that he was well known on Broadway and preferred it to Hollywood. I felt that it was part of his acting but he explained that you seldom know who the person is that is seeking you out and it could be someone who you might need at some time in the future. Show business seemed to me to be a very cutthroat business, controlled by the whims of some very emotional and self-important people. That was the opinion of a four-week expert!

The main supporting actors were people that I had seen on the screen before and recognized their faces and voices yet couldn't put a name to them. I learned that there was a large contingent of supporting actors who work a lot, make a lot of money, but never seem to make the leading parts in the show. Whether it is their agent's fault, their lack of desire for stardom, or just not quite having the glamour appeal needed for capturing a public following, I couldn't tell. The actors who had been chosen for this movie had all worked for John London before and I guess it was a sign of job security when you worked for a "winner" and he recognized you as part of the reason for his successes.

Shooting a film before the use of video cameras was a

trying and lengthy process. They would set up the scene and shoot it with all of the actors playing their parts while cameras covered them from several different angles. The director and assistant directors all discussed whether they thought the take was good or not after it was finished. Blown lines or movements were cause for stopping and starting over again. Sometimes the director didn't like the way a scene or action looks as it unfolded in front of him on the set and he stopped the shooting. Other times the actor might stop and make a suggestion as to how he thinks it would be more appropriately done.

After a scene was completed to the director's satisfaction, a close-up of each of the actors was taken. The actor being photographed acts out his role just as he did in the "whole scene" shoot and the other actors with talking parts read their lines from off camera. This process is repeated with each of the participating actors until all of them appearing in the scene have been shot "close-up." Every aspect of the scene is essential and the script girl, make-up artist, lighting manager, chief grip (who places the microphones and sound equipment) and all of the assistants are closely involved with each scene. They all have a controlling part in the acceptance or rejection of all or part of each scene. It is amazing that anything can slip by all of this close observation, but it does.

I was watching a scene that was being shot for the sixth or seventh time. The set in which I was sitting was made up for a re-shoot of a scene from another show. The female star had come in and sat down next to me on the bed where I was seated. It was just out of the camera coverage and I could watch and hear everything the actors were doing without being in the way. The very pretty lady that sat next to me made some small comments during the breaks but was not really interested in carrying on a conversation. Following a long scene, one of the actors ripped the telephone wire out of the wall in a fit of anger. A little later in the scene, another actor ran to the phone to make an emergency call.

During the first few shootings, some suggestions and changes had altered the original script. I was not involved and was sitting in an adjacent darkened set watching the action. When I heard John Newland say, "That's a wrap," I went over to him and told him what I had observed. No one believed it had happened until the actors involved joined the discussion and confirmed that one had torn the phone out of the wall and the other had used it a short time later. I wasn't exactly winning a popularity contest with all of the crew but they knew someone would undoubtedly catch it in the screening room and they would have to set up all over again and re-shoot the scene. When I returned to my seat on the bed, Gloria DeHaven said "You're for real. You're not an actor." From that point on she was very friendly and very much into talking about flying and Edwards Air Force Base. I realized then, that Bob DeHaven, the chief test pilot at Hughes Aircraft Company was her brother.

At the end of a very long 10 days of actual shooting, we completed the final screening and left the studio at 2:00 A.M. on Saturday night for a short celebration. They had asked me how I wanted my name to appear in the credits. I said that I didn't feel that it should be there as I was not in the profession and suggested they put the name of one of the people whose name would normally not appear. I was glad to return to my desert home and back to the real world but I can say to this day that it was a very interesting insight into the world of well paid make believe.

On my next large non-flying program, I was given the assignment to manage the five world record attempts by the Navy, the Tactical Air Command, the Air Defense Command, the Strategic Air Command and the Aeronautical Research and Development Command. These were all flown from Edwards Air Force Base using all facilities available to verify these world records. All of the attempts were to be made from the runway at Edwards AFB and the Flight Test Center had been handed the support and coordination of all events by the Department of Defense.

MacDonnell Aircraft Company had been working with the Navy on setting the altitude record with the F-4H and lost one of their test pilots while working on the performance profile. He made the run to Mach 2 and the pull-up into the zoom climb that took the aircraft to its maximum altitude, arriving there with all of its energy spent. It appeared that the aircraft went into a flat spin at somewhere in the vicinity of 100,000 feet and the pilot was unable to get it out of the spin. The F-4 impacted in the mountains near Gorman, California and the pilot must not have realized how high the ground elevation was in the area as he appeared to have ejected at too low an altitude and did not survive. The Navy's test pilot, Commander Don Engen, was assigned to make the official record attempts but for almost a month he had problems with the engines not being peaked to perfection and could not quite reach the altitude needed to break the Russian records by the required percentage. It made it more difficult each time the record was set as the percentage required was a fixed number and the larger the altitude number reached, the greater the number of feet above that number had to be.

My job was mainly to make certain that all of the facilities needed to support these attempts were provided from resources at Edwards, and to coordinate with the international body that observes and validates all world record events. I was given all of the assistance the Flight Test Center could provide for them. Commander Engen had to leave the project due to another assignment and a Commander Larry Flint took over the record attempts. I don't remember how many official runs were made before they got everything right and Larry set the new world altitude record. After the record was returned to the United States by the F-4H Phantom, it was superseded in just a few short weeks by Captain Joe Jordan from Fighter Test Operations at Edwards in an F-104. The closed course record was run in an F-101A and established by a Colonel Taylor from the Strategic Air Command. General Joe Moore from the Tactical Air Command established another world speed record in the F-105 and Colonel Joe Rogers from the Air Defense Command set a straight away speed record in the F-106. This was all accomplished in a matter of just a few weeks and I was proud to have been a small part of the outstanding effort put forth by all parties concerned.

Another thing about my grounding was that I spent a little more time with my family and enjoyed that time, even though I was frustrated at not being up there in the sky with every aircraft I saw taking off and landing. I was home when Tracy fell off her bicycle and the seat spring ripped a deep cut in her leg. Dr. Eddie Saickes came to the rescue again and sewed it up while I tried to watch and had to go sit down and put my head between my knees to keep from passing out. It was hard watching that little girl have such an awful looking injury but she took it a lot better than I did. Kerry had her problems also and I remember one bad fall she had out of bed where she landed on her nose and looked like a boxer for several days.

Both girls started their formal education at the base elementary school and were fairly lucky compared to many military children, in that they did not have to transfer every two or three years to a different school. We moved back to Dayton and then to Berwyn, PA where Tracy finished high school. Kerry wasn't as lucky and suffered the trauma of having to spend her high school years in three different schools, Melbourne High and the University of Florida; Government School at the Island Kingdom of Bahrain; and The American School in Lugano, Switzerland. On the isolated base at Edwards they made good friends and still laugh when they see the annual New Year's Day parade movies that they performed each New Year's morning with some other neighborhood children. It was a time that forced Evie and me to get up when we would rather have been sleeping, but we did our duty along with the other parents to take movies and admire the ingenuity of the young minds in their float designs.

Another job that I inherited away from the flight line was helping to prepare farewell parties for departing test pilots. My legacy, which I believe is still in place, was my preparing a photo album with pictures of all of the test pilots who were assigned to flight test during the period that the departing pilot was there. We gave them a very nice white leather covered album with a metal flight test center crest mounted on the front.

During my recovery I was able to fly my Cessna 195B all over the west on Air Force business and pleasure. It wasn't a fighter but I was back in the environment that I loved and felt that I belonged!

Dr. Karo was the commander of the Edwards AFB hospital and was the only doctor willing to go out on a limb to recommend that I be returned to flight status. The process required lots of bureaucratic paperwork that had to pass through the Surgeon General's office at Air Research and Development Command Headquarters and then had to be reviewed by the United States Surgeon General's office. There was a board that met in Washington, DC every month to review and pass on medical requests for disability retirements, return to flight status and such. My paperwork kept being bounced back to me for some typing error, wrong office symbol and all sorts of meaningless excuses to pass on my request. I'm reasonably certain that someone felt that I would give up and take my disability retirement and they would not have to stick their necks out by returning me to flying.

I finally got permission to fly on our courier flight to ARDC Headquarters in Baltimore and hand carry my paperwork. General Don Flickenger was the Surgeon General for ARDC and sat on the U.S. Surgeon General's Board. My overworked "Guardian Angel" was helping me again as I was waiting in the lobby at headquarters when he came in and recognized me. When I explained why I was there he said that if I was so dedicated that I was fighting so hard to get back to doing a dangerous job such as flight testing for our government when I could retire and then get a good paying job flying for one of the aircraft companies, he would personally take my paperwork. He told me he would take it with him to the next Surgeon General's meeting. He took my package and three weeks later my good friend Jim Butler, who was now assigned to Headquarters at the Flight Test Center, brought me the good news that I was returned to full flight status!

My time after getting back on flying status was very productive but the commanders were a little reluctant to put me on any exotic "X" Model project as the veil of potential cancer returning limited their decision-making in my favor. I really didn't notice, as I was so happy to be back in the saddle that I started back at "full afterburner!" I flew everything and every type of test flight that was available to me. I had flown with other test pilots on chase flights in the back seat of the T-33, F-104D, F-100F, and TF-86F before my return to flight status orders came through. When they did, I flew one flight with 10 landings in the T-33 and then a formation flight in an F-86F on which I proved to myself and to Don Sorlie, the lead pilot, that I could still fly formation acrobatics. That certified me for returning to chase flight status. I participated in all of the test programs that were in progress such as the F-100D and F-104C/D Phase VI testing. The first test program that was given to me was the F-101B stability, control, and I ended up with the performance program when the assigned pilot was killed in a U-2 crash.

I took over "Deke" Slayton's F-105B test program when he was selected as a Mercury astronaut. My first flight test program on a newly designed fighter came in early 1959 when I was assigned to the Northrop N-156F, which became the F-5A when a production contract was awarded. After being made Commander of "A" section, Fighter Test Operations, I was given the Category #I test on the F-104G and that was followed by my commanding the International Flight Test Operations for the Category II Flight Test of the F-104G. That was followed by being the Flight Test Advisor to the Category-III for the F-104G in Germany. I was sent to Vietnam as an evaluation test pilot who flew all of the Air Force, Army and South Vietnam aircraft flying combat in 1963 and returned with recommendations as to a replacement for the A-1A Sky

Raiders and T-28's. I left Edwards AFB to return to Wright-Patterson AFB to become Commander of the Fighter Test Operations Division in spring 1963. My extended time here on Earth also allowed me to be the only U.S. participant in the NATO Air Show in Brussels, Belgium while putting on an acrobatic display in an aircraft in which I had only three previous flights. For this, I received many accolades.

I retired from the United States Air Force in 1966 to start a new career by becoming a company Astronaut for General Electric on its MOL Project (Manned Orbiting Laboratory). I thought I had pretty much "done it all" when I left the military, but the next 26 years working as a civilian test pilot were filled with exciting and rewarding adventures. I realize when thinking back over my life, many of my amazing opportunities would never have been possible without my Guardian Angel working overtime, my amazing doctors, and the support of so many incredible friends and family.

EPILOGUE

I believe it is fitting that people who enjoy their freedom today and can live and think as they want without really having to put anything into defending that luxury, should know what other people have been willing to do to make that possible for them. Everyone knows that throughout history people have died fighting for what they or their masters believed in. Very little can be done for those people, except to honor them on Memorial Day with parades and prayers of thanks.

There is another type of dedication that is sometimes forgotten and that is the selfless dedication that the men and women who have sworn to protect our country display every day. They are the quiet heroes who are willing to lay down their lives so we can continue to enjoy all the freedoms we often take for granted.

GLOSSSARY

Aeleron: *the hinged surface in the trailing edge of an airplane wing, used to control lateral balance.*

AOCP: out of commission for lack of available part.

Attitude: Reference to an aircraft's position with respect to the horizon.

ARDC: Air Research and Development Command.

Azimuth: the direction of a celestial object from the observer, expressed as the angular distance from the north or south point of the horizon to the point at which a vertical circle passing through the object intersects the horizon. The horizontal angle or direction of a compass bearing.

Bikini: Bikini Atoll is an atoll in the Marshall Islands which consists of 23 islands totalling 3.4 square miles surrounding a deep 229.4-square-mile central lagoon. *(Wikipedia)*

CVE: Escort aircraft carrier. *(Wikipedia)*

D: Detonation

D-0: The day of scheduled detonation.

D-1: One day before day of scheduled detonation.

D-2: Two days before scheduled detonation.

Eniwetok: Eniwetok Atoll is a large coral atoll of 40 islands in the Pacific Ocean and with its 850 people forms a legislative district of the Ralik Chain of the Marshall Islands. *(Wikipedia)*

FTF: *Functional Test Flight.*

GCA: Ground Control Approach. A GCA is an instrument approach in which the actions of the pilot flying the airplane are directed by a ground radar controller.

H-Hour: The hour the bomb will be exploded.

Holmes and Narver: The company responsible for the basic services such as feeding, facility maintenance, etc. on Eniwetok.

MATS: Military Air Transport Service

M.O.S: Military Operational Specialty code These codes are used to identify particular jobs.

MSQ radar control: The Eniwetok precision radar control for the shots that were set off at Eniwetok.

NCO Club: Noncommissioned officer's club.

Operation Redwing: Operation Redwing was a United States series of 17 nuclear test detonations from May to July 1956. They were conducted at Bikini and Eniwetok atolls by Joint Task Force 7 (JTF7). All shots were named after various Native American tribes. *(Wikipedia)*

The author tested these shots which were code named:
Apache
Cherokee
Dakota
Flathead
Inca
Lacrosse
Mohawk
Navajo
Osage
Seminole
Zuni

Point zero. A position relative to the location of the bomb and a spot in space one needs to occupy at the instant the bomb was exploded.

Radist System: Radio navigation system in which the comparison of arrival times of transmitted pulsed, at three or more ground stations, indicates the position of the vehicle. *(The Free Dictionary)*

RAF: Royal Air Force—the United Kingdom's aerial warfare force. Formed towards the end of the First World War on 1 April 1918, it is the oldest independent air force in the world. *(Wikipedia)*

Snark Missile Program: The Northrop SM-62 Snark was an early-model intercontinental range ground-launched cruise missile that could carry a W39 thermonuclear warhead. The Snark was deployed by the United States Air Force's Strategic

Air Command from 1958 through 1961. It represented an important step in weapons technology during the Cold War.

The Snark missile was developed to present a nuclear deterrent to the Soviet Union and other potential enemies at a time when Intercontinental ballistic missiles (ICBMs) were still in development. The Snark was the only surface-to-surface cruise missile with such a long range that was ever deployed by the U.S. Air Force. Following the deployment of ICBMs, the Snark was rendered obsolete, and it was removed from deployment in 1961. *(Wikipedia)*

Sandia: Sandia National Laboratories is a Federally Funded Research and Development Center, whose facilities are owned by the U.S. government. Nuclear scientists from Sandia worked with the testing program on Eniwetok. *(Sandia.gov)*

T.A.C.: Tactical Air Command

TDY: Temporary Duty

Test clock time hack: Time synchronization.

The Rock: The Eniwetok Atoll

Time zero: The time of bomb detonation

T.O.: Technical Order

V.O.Q.: Visiting Officers Quarters

WADC: Wright Air Development Center, Wright-Patterson Air Force Base, Ohio.

WAF: Women's Air Force